THE MAGICAL
WORLDS OF
HARRY POTTER

Also by David Colbert:

Eyewitness to America: 500 Years of Firsthand History
Eyewitness to the American West
Eyewitness to Wall Street
Baseball: The National Pastime in Art and Literature
WWII: A Tribute in Art and Literature

THE MAGICAL WORLDS OF HARRY POTTER

A Treasury of Myths,
Legends, and Fascinating Facts

DAVID COLBERT

LUMINA PRESS

The Magical Worlds of Harry Potter: A Treasury of
Myths, Legends, and Fascinating Facts by David Colbert

Published in the United States by
Lumina Press LLC
P.O. Box 1106
Wrightsville Beach, NC 28480
www.luminapress.com

Library of Congress Control Number: 2001089759

ISBN: 0-9708442-0-4
Printed in the United States of America
First Edition

1 2 3 4 5 6 7 8 9 0

For my nieces Emma, Lillian, and Molly, and my nephew Sam

Read myths with the eyes of wonder:
the myths transparent to their universal meaning,
their meaning transparent to its mysterious source.

The first of Joseph Campbell's
Ten Commandments for Reading Mythology

Contents

Guide to abbreviations of the book titles:

Harry Potter and the Sorcerer's Stone (US title),
Harry Potter and the Philosopher's Stone (British title)*: Stone*

Harry Potter and the Chamber of Secrets: Chamber

Harry Potter and the Prisoner of Azkaban: Azkaban

Harry Potter and the Goblet of Fire: Goblet

Fantastic Beasts and Where to Find Them: Beasts

Quidditch Through the Ages: Quidditch

Introduction

ONE OF THE PLEASURES OF READING J. K. ROWLING IS discovering the playful references to history, legend, and literature that she hides in her books. For instance, the Sphinx in the maze during the Triwizard Tournament asks a riddle, just as the Sphinx of ancient Greek mythology did. Hagrid's pet dog Fluffy is actually another famous beast from Greek mythology, Cerberus. "Durmstrang," the name of the wizarding school that admits only full-blooded wizards and has questionable links to Lord Voldemort, comes from a German artistic style called *Sturm und Drang*, which was a favorite of Nazi Germany. As well, Durmstrang students arrive at Hogwarts in a ship like the one featured prominently in a famous *Sturm und Drang* opera. Alert readers know Rowling also hides fun clues in the names she chooses for characters. Draco, Harry's nemesis, gets his name from the Latin word for "dragon" or "snake." Dumbledore's pet phoenix, Fawkes, gets his name from a historical figure linked to bonfires just as phoenixes are said to be reborn in fire.

This book decodes her clues to reveal the artfully hidden meanings. In an online chat with fans, she encouraged one reader who asked the origin of a particular phrase to "go and look it up. A little investigation is good for a person." That's what *The Magical Worlds of Harry Potter* is about: a little investigation, in a spirit of fun. The point is to entertain, amuse, and fascinate.

You may even be sharing a laugh with Rowling herself. As TIME magazine said when noting that Hogwarts caretaker Argus Filch gets his name from the Argus of Greek mythology, a watchman with a thousand eyes on his body, "it's the sort of touch that can prompt an author's inward smile."

If you've never noticed those clues, don't feel alone. One of Rowling's amazing gifts is her ability to toss them out without breaking stride in telling her story. For example, she's happy to make only a passing reference in *Harry Potter and the Prisoner of Azkaban* to a manticore—a nasty, man-eating, imaginary beast. Skipping the opportunity to describe that creature in detail takes discipline. But for Rowling, it's just a casual reference. Still, when you know what a manticore is, and that it has appeared in legends for thousands of years, Rowling's story is all the more satisfying.

J. R. R. Tolkien, author of *The Hobbit* and *The Lord of the Rings*, coined the term "cauldron of story" to describe an ever-cooking pot of ideas, themes, and characters from which every writer takes, and to which every writer adds. Though the fictional world created by J. K. Rowling is unique, it grows from a deep foundation of myths and folklore that have endured across distance and time. The popularity of Rowling's books testifies to the breadth of culture from which she draws many of her images, characters, and themes. This book reveals that broader realm to fans whose awareness has been awakened by reading Rowling. As you'll see, she creates something entirely new with the bits of material from which she draws; yet she remains remarkably true to the essence of each.

Did Alchemists Really Search for a Magic Stone?

JUST WHAT WERE ALCHEMISTS TRYING TO do? Did they accomplish anything, or did all their work disappear in a cloud of smoke?

Alchemy

Anyone who has read *Stone* knows that alchemy is an ancient mix of chemistry and magic. Alchemists tried to create gold from less valuable metals, and to concoct a potion that could cure all ills and make the drinker immortal.

The Arab world is credited with the origin of alchemy. The name comes from the Arab term *al-kimia*, which also gives us the word "chemistry." However, some historians say the root of that Arab word is the ancient Greek *Khmia*, which means "Egypt." They believe Egyptian alchemists may have existed long before the Arab world began the practice. In any case, alchemy actually developed all over the world, including China and India.

We tend to think of alchemists as greedy and overreaching, obsessed with wealth and immortality. But some people say their work laid the foundation for modern chemistry. Indeed, real scientists studied alchemy. Sir Isaac Newton, the physicist and mathematician, wrote millions of words on the subject. However, in keeping with tradition, Newton was secretive about his alchemy experiments—at one point urging another alchemist to keep "high silence" about the work.

Just as the Arab word *al-kimia* gives us the terms "alchemy" and "chemistry," Arab mathematics, once the most advanced in the world, offers another term we hear in classroom today: *al-gebr*. It means "equalize," which is what students do with the two sides of an equation in algebra.

THE METROPOLIS OF ALCHEMY

During the late 1500s two emperors hired the world's leading alchemists to work in the city

of Prague in what is now the Czech Republic. This led to a nickname for the city: "the Metropolis of Alchemy." Emperors, however, can be fickle. When a British alchemist, Edward Kelley, failed to create gold, he was thrown in a dungeon. Even the efforts of Britain's Queen Elizabeth I failed to win his release. He died trying to escape.

Of course, there were many frauds. A story is told of the arrival in Prague during that era of a stranger from Arabia, who invited the city's wealthiest men to a banquet where he promised to multiply the gold they brought. After gathering the offerings he prepared a mixture of chemicals and odd ingredients, such as eggshells and horse manure. This blend proved to be a stinkbomb, which permitted the charlatan a quick escape with the gold.

THE PHILOSOPHER'S STONE

One source calls the actual process followed by alchemists "hopelessly complicated." However, the basics were simple. According to the standard theory, all metals were a combination of mercury and sulfur. The more yellow the metal, the more sulfur in the mixture. So combining sulfur with mercury, in the right proportion and with the proper sequence of steps, would create gold.

The original title of the first adventure, *Harry Potter and the Philosopher's Stone*, appeared on books in the United Kingdom, Canada, Australia, and other territories. The term "Sorcerer's Stone" was invented by the American publisher because it seemed more exciting.

See also:

Flamel

Fluffy

Mirrors

Eventually, alchemists became frustrated with simple methods that did not work. They began to search for a magic ingredient, which they called the philosopher's stone. Some alchemists continued to believe the magic ingredient was simply sulfur. However, in *Stone* it is described as "blood-red," so Rowling probably had something more interesting in mind.

Who Was the Most Amazing Animagus?

ADDING *MAGUS*, THE LATIN WORD FOR "wizard," to *animal*, J. K. Rowling coined the term "Animagus": a wizard who can become an animal yet retain magical powers.

Animagus

The ability to transform into an animal is as old as legend. In Celtic mythology, transformation into stags, boars, swans, eagles, and ravens is common. Shamans in Native American cultures often transform into animals, usually birds.

One of the first wizards to display this ability was Proteus, of Greek mythology. He was a servant of Poseidon, god of the oceans. One of his special talents was the knowledge of past, present, and future. Unfortunately, this meant he was often being asked for predictions. To get away from people he would quickly transform into a variety of animals and terrifying creatures. Something that changes shape is still said to be "protean."

Eagle-man totem figure from the Haida of the Pacific Northwest.

DUELING ANIMAGI

Some of
J. K. Rowling's
Animagi:

**Minerva
McGonagall** can
be a cat.

James Potter
became a stag,
leading to his
nickname,
"Prongs."

Sirius Black,
whose name
means "black
dog," can be one.

Rita Skeeter can
become a beetle.

Peter Pettigrew,
"Wormtail,"
disguised himself
as Ron's pet
rat, Scabbers.

This sort of rapid-fire shape-shifting was remembered by the author T. H. White, whose novel *The Sword in the Stone* retells the legend of young King Arthur and his tutor, Merlin (spelled "Merlyn" by White). In that book, Merlin battles another sorcerer, Madame Mim, in one of the most imaginative duels in literature:

> The object of the wizard in the duel was to turn himself into some kind of animal, vegetable or mineral which would destroy the particular animal, vegetable or mineral which had been selected by his opponent. Sometimes it went on for hours. . . .
>
> At the first gong Madame Mim immediately turned herself into a dragon. It was the accepted opening move and

Merlyn ought to have replied by being a thunderstorm or something like that. Instead, he caused a great deal of preliminary confusion by becoming a field mouse, which was quite invisible in the grass, and nibbled Madame Mim's tail, as she stared about in all directions, for about five minutes before she noticed him. But when she did notice the nibbling, she was a furious cat in two flicks.

Wart [Arthur] held his breath to see what the mouse would become next—he thought perhaps a tiger which could kill the cat—but Merlyn merely became another cat. He stood opposite her and made faces. This most irregular procedure put Madame Mim quite out of her stride, and it took her more than a minute to regain her bearings and become a dog. Even as she became it, Merlyn was another dog standing opposite her, of the same sort.

"Oh, well played, sir!" cried the Wart, beginning to see the plan.

Madame Mim was furious. . . . She had better alter her own tactics and give Merlyn a surprise. . . .

She had decided to try a new tack by

T. H. White's Merlyn also changed Arthur into animals, to teach him each animal's skills.

leaving the offensive to Merlyn, beginning by assuming a defensive shape herself. She turned into a spreading oak.

Merlyn stood baffled under the oak for a few seconds. Then he most cheekily—and, as it turned out, rashly—became a powdery little blue-tit, which flew up and sat perkily on Madame Mim's branches. You could see the oak boiling with indignation for a moment; but then its rage became icy cold, and the poor little blue-tit was sitting, not on an oak, but on a snake. The snake's mouth was open, and the bird was actually perching on its jaws. As the jaws clashed

together, but only in the nick of time, the
bird whizzed off as a gnat into the safe
air. Madame Mim had got it on the run,
however, and the speed of the contest
now became bewildering. The quicker
the attacker could assume a form, the less
time the fugitive had to think of a form
which would elude it, and now the
changes were as quick as thought.

The battle ends when Madame Mim
changes herself into an aullay, an animal that
looks like an enormously large horse with the
trunk of an elephant. She charges at Merlyn,
but he simply disappears. Suddenly,

> . . . strange things began to happen. The
> aullay got hiccoughs, turned red, swelled
> visibly, began whooping, came out in
> spots, staggered three times, rolled its
> eyes, fell rumbling to the ground. It
> groaned, kicked and said Farewell. . . .
> The ingenious magician had turned
> himself successively into the microbes,
> not yet discovered, of hiccoughs, scarlet
> fever, mumps, whooping cough, measles
> and heat spots, and from a complication
> of all these complaints the infamous
> Madame Mim had immediately expired.

ROWLING'S RULES

A great difference between Rowling's world and that of nearly every other author is the restriction on Animagi. According to Rowling, this is a relatively rare ability, and highly regulated. The Ministry of Magic keeps a register of Animagi. But in nearly every other fictional world, wizards are capable of becoming any animal they please.

Perhaps Rowling is aware of the risks of taking animal form. In *Quidditch Through the Ages* she warns, "The witch or wizard who finds him- or herself transfigured into a bat may take to the air, but, having a bat's brain, they are sure to forget where they want to go the moment they take flight." Another famous writer, Ursula K. Le Guin, describes in a story titled *A Wizard of Earthsea* what can happen to wizards who aren't careful:

J. K. Rowling says one's personality is a factor in determining what animal one can become.
She adds, "I personally would like to think that I would transform into an otter, which is my favorite animal."

> As a boy, Ogion like all boys had thought it would be a very pleasant game to take by art-magic whatever shape one liked, man or beast, tree or cloud, and so to play at a thousand beings. But as a wizard he had learned the price of the game, which is the peril of losing one's self, playing away the truth. The longer a man stays in a form not his own, the greater

this peril. Every prentice-sorcerer learns the tale of the wizard Bordger of Way, who delighted in taking bear's shape, and did so more and more often until the bear grew in him and the man died away, and he became a bear, and killed his own little son in the forests, and was hunted down and slain. And no one knows how many of the dolphins that leap in the waters of the Inmost Sea were men once, wise men, who forgot their wisdom and their name in the joy of the restless sea.

No doubt Harry, who often pushes himself beyond the usual boundaries, will face this risk. But first we must wait to learn what sort of Animagus he will become.

See also:

Black, Sirius

McGonagall

Is "Avada Kedavra" a Real Curse?

IN HARRY'S WORLD, THIS IS THE KILLING curse, the worst of the three Unforgivable Curses, any of which can bring a life term in Azkaban for a wizard who uses it against another human. It is the curse that Lord Voldemort used to kill Harry's parents, the one with which he tried to kill Harry, and, sadly, the fatal blow to Cedric Diggory. Harry is the only person known to survive it.

Avada Kedavra

Although J. K. Rowling invents most of her spells and curses entirely from her imagination, the Avada Kedavra curse derives from a phrase in an ancient Middle Eastern language called Aramaic. That phrase, *abhadda kedhabhra*, meaning "disappear like this word," was used by ancient wizards to make illnesses disappear. However, there's no proof it was ever used to kill anyone.

The phrase is one likely origin of the magical word *abracadabra*. Now just part of a magician's entertaining chatter, that word was once used by doctors. Quintus Serenus Sammonicus, a Roman physician who lived about A.D. 200, used it as a spell to make fever vanish. According to his prescription, it was to be written eleven times on a piece of paper, with one letter "disappearing" each time:

ABRACADABRA
ABRACADABR
ABRACADAB
ABRACADA
ABRACAD
ABRACA
ABRAC
ABRA
ABR
AB
A

The paper was to be tied around the patient's neck with flax for nine days, then tossed over the shoulder into a stream running to the east. When the water dissolved the words, the fever would disappear. The popularity of this cure grew in the centuries after Sammonicus, and it was even used to make the Black Death disappear. Clever readers will notice that this remedy, if it does nothing else,

See also:

Latin

lets time pass. Because many diseases run their course naturally in a week or two, the spell probably did not do any good at all. On the other hand, it didn't hurt!

Are Basilisks Just Big Snakes?

BASILISKS ARE AMONG THE MOST DREADED magical creatures. "Of the many fearsome beasts and monsters that roam our land," Hermione reads in *Chamber*, "there is none more curious or more deadly."

Basilisks

The basilisk is certainly more than just a large snake. Also known as a cockatrice, it has existed in legend for centuries. Rowling is just having fun in *Beasts* when she credits a Greek wizard named Herpo the Foul with breeding the first basilisk. *Herpein* is a Greek word meaning "to creep" that came to be a word describing snakes. The study of reptiles such as snakes is now called herpetology.

However, just as she suggests, by legend the basilisk was said to be the offspring of a rooster or hen mated with a snake or toad. Some artists followed that description literally, and drew strange beasts combining features from those animals. But more often the basilisk was portrayed as a serpent with a crown or a white spot on his head. Cobras, which have such marks, may be the origin of the basilisk legend.

Basilisk, from an early woodcut and a later engraving.

The basilisk was reported to be deadly even from afar. The Roman naturalist Pliny said, "He kills the shrubs, not only by contact, but by breathing on them, and splits the rocks, such is the power of evil in him."

Humans who looked at the snaky head of **Medusa** were turned to stone.

Some sources describe three varieties: the golden basilisk could poison with a look; another sparked fire; a third, like the famous snaky hair of Medusa in Greek mythology, caused such horror that victims were petrified.

William Shakespeare even mentioned a basilisk in his play *Richard III*. The evil title character kills his brother then immediately flatters his brother's widow by mentioning her beautiful eyes. But she isn't interested in his compliments. She replies, "Would they were a basilisk's, to strike thee dead!"

HOW TO FIGHT A BASILISK

A basilisk controlled by Lord Voldemort slinks through Hogwarts in *Chamber*, almost killing Harry and several of his friends. Harry is saved from that basilisk by Fawkes, Professor Dumbledore's pet phoenix, who pecks the monster's eyes. It is fitting that a bird saves Harry. According to legend, a bird—the rooster—is fatal to the beast. In the Middle Ages travelers were known to carry roosters as protection against basilisks.

See also:

Beasts

Nagini

Spiders

Which "Fantastic Beasts" Come from Legend?

Beasts

MANY OF THE CREATURES IN THE TEXTBOOK *Fantastic Beasts and Where to Find Them* are known in our world as well as Harry's, even if they are legendary. Here are some of the stories from which J. K. Rowling drew:

The author of *Beasts*, Newton ("Newt") Artemis Fido Scamander, has a name filled with puns. Newts are small salamanders, the magical lizards that live in fire (see below). Artemis was the Greek god of hunting—appropriate for a scholar who looks for magical beasts. (Cont.)

RED CAP

According to *Beasts*, Red Caps "live in holes on old battlegrounds or wherever human blood has been spilled . . . [and] will attempt to bludgeon [Muggles] to death on dark nights." This creature has long existed in the legends of England and Scotland, neighbors who fought many gruesome wars. He is also known as Bloody Cap or Red Comb. His cap is red because he uses it to catch the blood of his victims.

RAMORA

True to a legend that goes back thousands of years, Rowling says this fish—which does

(Newt's name, cont.)
Fido, from the Latin *fidus* ("faithful"), is a common pet name. Scamander sounds like salamander, though it is actually the name of a river mentioned in Homer's account of the Trojan War, *The Iliad*. The river battled wth the hero Achilles, but was subdued by fire.

Hippocampus, from a Dutch woodcut.

exist and which we know as the remora—has the power to stop ships. In fact, the name remora comes from the Latin word for "delay." Using a suction cup on its head, it attaches itself to ships and sharks in order to feed on scraps. Also known as the Mora and Echeneis, its strength had already been exaggerated by the first century A.D., when Pliny the Elder wrote, "Gales may blow and storms may rage; this fish rules their fury, restrains their mighty strength, and brings vessels to a stop, a thing no cable can do, nor anchors. How futile a creature is man, who can be checked and held fast by a little fish six inches long!" Pliny claimed the ship of Marc Antony was anchored by remoras during the Battle of Actium, causing him to lose the battle and changing the course of Roman history.

HIPPOCAMPUS

This sea horse gets its name from the Greek word for horse (*hippos*) and the Latin word for ground (*campus*). It is also called the Hydrippus (the Greek word for "water" is *hydro*.) The chariot of the Greek sea-god Poseidon is pulled by hippocamps.

A book called the *Physiologus*, written about the second century A.D., says some legends deemed the Hippocampus "the king of all fishes." But by the time that book was written, Judaism and Christianity were pushing aside old myths, and the legend had changed slightly to incorporate the idea of a special golden fish living in the East. In that version, the hippocampus is a guide similar to Moses: "When the fish of the sea have met together and gathered themselves into flocks, they go in search of the Hydrippus; and when they have found him, he turns himself towards the East, and they all follow him, all the fish from the North and from the South; and they draw near to the golden fish, the Hydrippus leading them. And, when the Hydrippus and all the fish are arrived, they greet the golden fish as their King."

SALAMANDER

Rowling says these are "fire-dwelling" lizards that live "only as long as the fire from which they sprang burns." This legend goes back thousands of years. The Greek philosopher Aristotle wrote in the fourth century B.C. that "the fact that certain animals cannot be burnt is evidenced by the salamander, which puts out a fire by crawling through it." It could do this because it was said to be extremely cold. Almost a thousand years later St. Isidore, Bishop of Seville, agreed that the salamander

Salamander in flames, from a family crest.

"lives in the midst of flames without pain and without being consumed," adding, "amid all poisons its power is the greatest. Other poisonous animals strike individuals, but this slays many at the same time by crawling up a tree and infecting the fruit, killing all those who eat it."

ERKLING

Rowling has transposed a few letters in the name of the Erl King or Erl König ("elf king") of German legend. Otherwise, her description holds true. It is an evil creature in the Black Forest of Germany that tries to snatch children. In Johann Wolfgang von Goethe's poem "Erl King" it calls out to a young boy who is traveling through the woods with his father:

> *"Oh, come, thou dear infant! Oh, come thou with me!*
> *Full many a game I will play there with thee."*

Although the boy tries to warn his father (who can't hear the Erl King), the poem ends badly. Like legends of grindylows in England and kappas in Japan, the story of the Erl King was concocted by parents to prevent children from wandering.

Today many restaurants have special ovens called **salamanders**, so named because their long, thin heating elements are curved like a snake or lizard's tail and are extremely hot.

CHIMAERA

The description of the Chimaera in *Beasts*, odd as it sounds, is true to the early Greek legend of a monster with three heads—one of a dragon, one of a lion, another of a goat. It is a sibling of both the Sphinx and Cerberus, the three-headed dog that guarded the Underworld.

Rowling casually mentions "there is only one known instance of the successful slaying of a Chimaera and the unlucky wizard concerned fell to his death from his winged horse." She is playing with the original legend, in which the monster was slain by the hero Bellerophon, who rode the winged horse Pegasus. Bellerophon survived that battle; but in a later adventure, when he arrogantly attempted to ride the horse to Mount Olympus, home of the gods, Zeus punished him by throwing him off Pegasus and crippling him.

The **Chimaera**, from a fifth century B.C. bronze decoration.

The term "chimaera" has come to mean something (usually a living creature) created by humans by artificially combining things that occur in nature.

KELPIE

As described in *Beasts*, this Celtic water demon is usually seen as a horse with a mane of green rushes. It lures people onto its back, then drags them into deep water. As Rowling says, bridling a kelpie will subdue it. Because it is supernaturally strong, it can do the work of many horses.

SELKIES AND MERROWS

In the entry for merpeople in *Beasts*, Rowling mentions selkies and Merrows. These are specific sorts of merpeople known in Britain. The selkies are seal people of the country's northern islands. They can assume very beautiful humans forms, but must resume their seal form in the water. To kill a selkie is to invite a disastrous storm. Merrows are from Ireland. The women are beautiful but the men are quite ugly. They are said to have magic hats, and if a human can steal the hat the merrow will not be able to return to the sea.

See also:

Boggarts

Cornish Pixies

Grindylows

Kappas

Merpeople

Veela

Why Would Sirius Black Become a Black Dog?

S IRIUS BLACK, HARRY'S GODFATHER, IS A fugitive from the Ministry of Magic, which mistakenly believes he is a Death Eater. He was able to escape Azkaban because he is an Animagus. He changed into his dog form, squeezed through the bars of his cell, and swam to his freedom.

Black, Sirius

THE DOG STAR

As an Animagus form, a black dog suits him perfectly. The name "Sirius" comes from the name of a star often referred to as the Dog Star. It has that nickname because it is in the constellation known as the Great Dog. (The star was given the name "Sirius" because it is the brightest star in the sky. The Greek word *seirios* means "burning.")

That star has great significance in the magical world. As the symbol of the goddess Isis, it was central to the religion and philosophy of Egypt, where most magic originated.

The Egyptian goddess **Isis**.

The Egyptians used Sirius to set their calendar, because its movements are linked to the seasons. On the first day of summer, it rises just before the sun. That was New Year's Day in ancient Egypt. It forecast the annual flooding of the Nile River, which gave vital nourishment to the growing fields. We refer to the long, hot days of summer now as "dog days" because Sirius marks their arrival.

According to the Egyptians, Sirius was not merely significant to life on Earth. As one Egyptologist puts it, Sirius was "the home of departed souls." The star was so important that temples were built to align with its path across the sky. One archaeologist determined that the long tunnels or airshafts in the Great Pyramid make the stars visible in daytime, and that the view is that part of the sky where

Sirius appears. Another says "these openings were meant to be guide ways for the soul."

PADFOOT

The Animagus form of a black dog is appropriate to Sirius Black in more than name alone. Magical black dogs appear mysteriously throughout Europe and North America. There have been many sightings in Britain, where they are known by names like Black Shuck (from the Anglo-Saxon *scucca*, meaning "demon"), Old Shuck, Shucky Dog, the Shug Monster and Shag Dog. The residents of Staffordshire in central England gave it the name Sirius uses: Padfoot.

Some say the dogs guard churchyards or certain roads; others say they roam the countryside at night. Eyewitnesses say they appear suddenly, sometimes right alongside a person walking alone. They tend to be larger than usual dogs. They may vanish in an instant, or slowly fade from view while standing still. Occasionally they appear without heads. Their eyes are almost always described as huge and "blazing." Surprisingly, they tend to be silent.

Scholars were once convinced that the black dog was the preferred form of the Devil. Even among people with less anxious minds,

The origin of "**Snuffles**," the name Sirius asks Harry to call him when referring to him in casual conversation with Ron and Hermione, is unknown. Perhaps he believes it is unlikely to draw the attention of eavesdroppers because it does not fit his dangerous reputation.

black dogs are widely feared. Many consider them an omen of death. This is precisely what Professor Trelawney tells Harry his early sightings of Sirius mean. (She refers to the black dog as the Grim, another common name.)

The eyewitness reports go back many hundreds of years. One vivid account from 1577 describes the arrival of a black dog in church: "There appeared in a most horrible form a dog of a black color, together with fearful flashes of fire which made some in the assembly think doomsday was come. This dog, or the Devil in such a likeness, ran the length of the church with great swiftness and incredible haste, passed between two persons as they were kneeling and wrung the necks of them both at one instant."

That may have been an especially horrible incident. Not every encounter is so awful. In more recent sightings the black dog seems to have become less malevolent. One scholar says, "There is rather more evidence that black dogs are friendly (or at least harmless) than that they are dangerous. Indeed the dogs are often positively helpful."

Whether or not this helpful black dog is Sirius Black is impossible to know.

See also:
Animagus
Egypt
McGonagall

Which Creature Doesn't Know When to Say Good-bye?

SOME MAGICAL CREATURES CAN BE MORE dangerous than others. A boggart might seem dangerous at first, because, as Hermione explains in *Azkaban*, it can "take the shape of whatever it thinks will frighten us most." But more than anything else, boggarts are annoying.

Boggarts

These are the same creatures known as "bogeys" or "bogeymen" in the United States, "bogle" in Scotland, and "Boggelmann" in Germany. Sometimes said to be mistreated spirits that have become malevolent, boggarts love mischief and usually aren't very harmful. They like to come out at night, when they can be most convincing.

From the words *bogey* and *boggart* we also get names of less frightening annoyances like "**bugaboo**" and "**bugbear**."

Often they are house spirits, and in those cases the only way to get rid of them is to move. This is easier said than done, as a boggart will sometimes take the trouble to move with a household it finds particularly entertaining. The more frustrated the family becomes, the more fun the boggart has.

See also:

Beasts

Cornish Pixies

Goblins

Trolls

Veela

Harry faces boggarts in *Azkaban* and in the maze in *Goblet*. He defeats them with advice from Professor Lupin that sounds like what children in our world have been told for centuries: "The thing that really finishes a boggart is laughter." Of course, this is easier for wizards, who can simply use the Riddikulus charm to turn the boggart into something funny.

Have Witches Always Flown on Broomsticks?

BY LEGEND, BROOMSTICKS ARE THE MOST common means of transportation for witches. A popular American writer of the 19th century, Oliver Wendell Holmes, penned this rhyme on the subject:

Broomsticks

In Essex county there's many a roof
Well known to him of the cloven hoof;
The small square windows are full in view
Which the midnight hags went sailing
*   through,*
On their well-trained broomsticks
*   mounted high,*
Seen like shadows against the sky;
Crossing the track of owls and bats,
Hugging before them their coal-black cats.

Women were more likely than men to use this means of travel, perhaps because the broom is used for domestic chores, which men avoided. Sorcerers, when they did fly, tended to ride on pitchforks. For reasons never explained, witches in Europe and America were seen flying more often than those in Britain.

Witches were rumored to rub their broomsticks with a magical ointment to make them fly. Then, according to legend, they rode straight out of the chimney. This may be just a colorful exaggeration, derived from the real practice of pushing a broom up a chimney to let neighbors know one was away from home. Still, it sounds a bit like traveling by floo powder.

If villagers suspected that witches were flying about they would ring church bells, which reportedly had the power to knock witches off broomsticks.

Witches were sometimes accused of flying out to sea to create a storm.

One witch has emerged from the chimney on her broomstick, and another is halfway up it, in this sixteenth-century woodcut.

Why Do Centaurs Avoid Humans?

Centaurs

CENTAURS ARE MYTHICAL BEASTS WITH THE legs and bodies of horses, but with human torsos, arms, and heads. In *Beasts*, J. K. Rowling says "they prefer to live apart from wizards and Muggles alike." This fits the ancient legends. According to those stories, centaurs come from the mountains of Greece, where their relations with the local people were rather mixed. Because some centaurs were fond of wine, they tended to be boisterous, wild, and quick to anger. They fought many battles with humans. The most famous skirmish followed a wedding at which the centaurs, as usual, had celebrated a little too enthusiastically. They tried to carry off the bride, which led to a great war. (The centaurs lost.) Scenes from that war were a favorite decoration of Greek potters.

Centaur, from a second-century A.D. sarcophagus.

However, some centaurs were recognized to be noble. Chiron, having been taught arts such as medicine and hunting by the gods

Apollo and Artemis, founded a school where he taught some of the great heroes of the time, including Achilles and Odysseus.

LOST IN THE STARS

Although Chiron was immortal, a wound from a poisoned arrow threatened to cause him unceasing agony. Instead, he chose death. But Zeus, in recognition of Chiron's benevolence, placed him in the stars as the constellation Sagittarius. Another constellation, Centaurus, is one of the most visible in the Southern Hemisphere. Two of its stars, Alpha Centauri and Beta Centauri, are among the ten brightest in the sky. Alpha Centauri is the closest star to the Earth and the Sun. It is just over 4.3 light-years away. These heavenly connections may explain why the centaurs who live in the Forbidden Forest near Hogwarts—Firenze, Ronan, and Bane—look to the stars to read the future.

The centaur **Nessos**, foe of the hero Hercules. This drawing appeared on a Greek amphora (vase) in the 7th century B.C.

What Is the Favorite Trick of Cornish Pixies?

PIXIES ARE ENERGETIC HOUSEHOLD SPIRITS from the legends of southwestern England, which includes Cornwall. Most stories depict them dressed in green, wearing a pointed cap. They have youthful faces, and many have red hair. J. K. Rowling departs from tradition in *Chamber* and *Beasts*, describing them as "electric blue and about eight inches high."

Cornish Pixies

In folklore, pixies are often said to act like the house elves of Harry's world. They can be quite helpful but will disappear if given a gift of clothes. Unlike house elves, who are happy to do all the work, pixies will nip at lazy members of a household.

Pixies love to dance under the moonlight. At times they also take horses from stalls and ride them all night, returning them exhausted—and with mysteriously knotted manes—in the morning. But their favorite activity is to lead travelers astray. People who have lost their way (or are in any way bewildered or confused) are said to be "pixie-led." This disorienting spell may be broken by taking off one's jacket and putting it on again, inside-out.

Leading travelers off a path is a trick often played by another English spirit mentioned in *Azkaban*, the Hinky-Punk. Because it seems more like a misty cloud than a solid creature, some people call it the Will o' the Wisp.

See also:

Beasts

Boggarts

Why Would Voldemort Put the Dark Mark on Death Eaters?

THE DARK MARK IS THE FEARSOME SIGN OF Lord Voldemort. After the Quidditch World Cup in *Goblet*, "Something vast, green, and glittering erupted from the patch of darkness. . . . It was a colossal skull, comprised of what looked like emerald stars, with a serpent protruding from its mouth like a tongue." The symbol also appears on the arms of Voldemort's followers, growing more visible as Voldemort gains strength and draws near.

The Dark Mark is Voldemort's version of the Devil's Mark, a notion from the Middle Ages. According to one medieval demonologist, "the Devil makes a mark on them, especially those whose allegiance he suspects. The mark varies in shape and size; sometimes it is like a hare, sometimes like the foot of a toad, sometimes like a spider, a puppy, or a dormouse. It is imprinted on the most secret parts of the body; men may have it under their eyelids or armpits, on the lips or shoulders;

Dark Mark

"**Morsmorde**," the command that makes the Dark Mark appear, means "take a bite out of death" in French, making it a fitting call for Death Eaters.

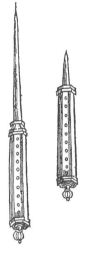

Bodkins like these were used to prick alleged witches, to test for the **Devil's Mark**. This illustration shows a trick bodkin. Its blade collapses into the handle.

See also:

Broomsticks

Voldemort

women generally have it on their breasts or private parts. The stamp that makes these marks is nothing less than the Devil's talon."

Witch hunters often declared scars, birthmarks, warts, or other blemishes to be the Devil's Mark. Accused witches were shaved completely so that every bit of their bodies could be examined.

In addition to the Devil's Mark, witch hunters would look for a Witch's Mark. This was a less serious matter—only the Devil's Mark signified a special pact, such as the bond between Voldemort and the Death Eaters—but it could still be fatal for the accused person. Every witch was believed to have one. Any blemish, like a mole or large freckle, might be identified as such.

Sometimes the Witch's Mark was said to be a spot of skin that did not bleed and where no pain could be felt, so accused witches were pricked with pins (called bodkins) as a test. Often, witch hunters were paid only if they found a witch; so many cheated. For instance, they used special bodkins, similar to the trick knives used in magicians' acts today. The sharp stem would disappear into the handle when pressed against someone, so it would not puncture the skin.

Why Would Chocolate Help after Escaping a Dementor?

Dementors

D EMENTORS, AS EVERY HARRY POTTER fan knows, are deadly magical creatures. Faceless, wearing shapeless cloaks that cover skin that is "grayish, slimy-looking, and scabbed," Dementors "drain peace, hope, and happiness out of the air around them" (*Azkaban*).

J. K. ROWLING'S EXPLANATION

Speaking to an interviewer, J. K. Rowling confirmed that Dementors represent the mental illness known as depression: "That is exactly what they are. It was entirely conscious. And entirely from my own experience. Depression is the most unpleasant thing I have ever experienced. It is that absence of being able to envisage that you will ever be cheerful again. The absence of hope. That very deadened feeling, which is so very different from feeling sad. Sad hurts but it's a healthy feeling. It's a necessary thing to feel. Depression is very different."

One can't help but notice that the remedy offered to lighten the effects of Dementors is chocolate, which doctors say can make depressed people feel better. The chocolate has some of the same effects as the medicine that doctors prescribe. Of course, chocolate does seem to be a cure for nearly every ill in Harry's world!

Is Sibyll Trelawney Ever Right?

Divination

P ROF. TRELAWNEY'S SUBJECT, DIVINATION, IS the interpretation of signs and actions to predict the future, look into the past, or, sometimes, simply find lost objects.

Many different methods are used for divination. The Romans favored augury, interpreting the flight of birds. Other cultures use hepatoscopy, examining the insides of sacrificed animals.

Not coincidentally, Ms. Trelawney's first name comes from the famous prophets of mythology, the Sibyls, who often offered their visions without even having been asked a question. Sibyll Trelawney is similarly inclined to assert predictions—often dreadful ones— without being asked. She predicts Harry's death soon after meeting him. But as Professor McGonagall says, "Sibyll Trelawney has predicted the death of one student a year since she arrived at this school. None of them has died yet."

Other types of divination, and what is studied:

Belomancy: the flight of arrows

Chiromancy: the lines of the hand

Dactylomancy: the swinging of a suspended ring (cont.)

Divination (con't):

Daphnomancy:
the crackling of
burning laurel

Geloscopy:
laughter

Lampadomancy:
a lamp flame

Libranomancy:
incense smoke

Lithomancy:
gemstones

Margaritomancy:
pearls

Metoposcopy:
forehead wrinkles

Phrenology:
shape of the skull

right: a chart for
reading palms.

J. K. Rowling seems skeptical of divination, or at least ambivalent. Hermione finds it "very woolly"—yet she is fond of arithmancy, which is divination from numbers. The centaurs in the Forbidden Forest are obsessed with reading what is fated in the stars, but they seem intelligent. Perhaps Rowling feels as Dumbledore explains to Harry in *Azkaban*: "The consequences of our actions are always so complicated, so diverse, that predicting the future is a very difficult business indeed."

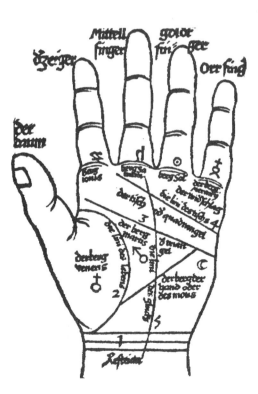

Which Creature Is Fit for a King?

Dragons

RAGONS (FROM THE LATIN *DRACO*—JUST like Draco Malfoy) are probably the best-known magical creatures in literature. Usually dangerous and terrifying, they are often the most challenging foe a hero can face. Literary critic John Clute notes this rule of ancient epics: "To kill a dragon is to become a king." As a result the dragon is the symbol of many real and fictional kings, including the legendary King Arthur, whose last name, Pendragon, means "head of the dragon" or "chief dragon." His golden helmet bore a dragon design.

Dragon on a royal crest.

However, as some heroes discover, dragons are often misunderstood. Though they can be frightening, they can also be benevolent.

UGLINESS IS ONLY SKIN DEEP

Many people fear dragons simply because of their appearance. This description from about

600 A.D. was taken very seriously:

J. R. R. Tolkien, author of *The Lord of the Rings*, explained why he liked writing about dragons: "The dragon had the trade-mark *Of Faërie* written plain upon him. In whatever world he had his being it was an Other-world. I desired dragons with a profound desire."

The dragon is the largest of all serpents and of all living things upon earth. It has a small face and narrow blow-holes through which it draws its breath and thrusts out its tongue. Being dragged from caves it rushes into the air, and the air is thrown into commotion on account of it. And it has its strength not in its teeth but in its tail, and it is dangerous for its stroke, rather than for its jaws. It is harmless in the way of poison, but poison is not necessary for it to cause death, because it kills whatever it has entangled in its folds. And from it the elephant is not safe because of its size. It grows in Ethiopia and in India, in the very burning of perennial heat.

It is easy to see why the dragon is often a symbol of destruction. That idea goes back thousands of years. In the New Testament, the Lord warns, "I will make Jerusalem heaps, and a den of dragons; and I will make the cities of Judah desolate, without an inhabitant."

BRITISH DRAGONS

Dragons play a big part in the legends of

Harry's homeland. For instance, they foretold one of the most important moments in British history. According to an official chronicle, the year A.D. 793 "began with ominous signs over Northumbria [one of the seven kingdoms of Britain at the time], and these utterly panicked the people. Huge streaks of flame rushed across the full length of the sky, and flaming dragons as well were seen flying through the air, bringing fierce hunger with them. And not long after that, on 8 June of this same year, ravaging heathens ruthlessly leveled God's Church in Lindisfarne [a village on the coast] with shameless robbing and butchering of men." Those "ravaging heathens" were Norsemen from Scandinavia. True to what had been foretold, their ships

were decorated to look like dragons. They continued to dominate Britain for hundreds of years.

Not surprisingly, the saint later adopted as the patron of England, St. George, is famous for slaying a dragon—symbolically defeating the foreigners. In *The Faerie Queen*, a famous poem written during the reign of Queen Elizabeth I, poet Edmund Spenser describes the dragon faced by the "Red-Cross Knight":

> *His body was monstrous, horrible, and vast,*
> *Swollen with wrath and poison and with*
>   *bloody gore;*
> *And over all with brazen scales was armed,*
> *Like plated coat of steel, that nothing*
>   *might pierce it,*
> *Nor could his body be harmed with dint of*
>   *sword, nor push of pointed spear.*
> *His wings were like two sails in which the*
>   *hollow wind*
> *Is gathered full, and work speedy way.*
> *His huge long tail, wound up in hundred folds,*
> *Spread across his long back.*
> *Spotted with scales of red and black,*
> *It sweeps all the land behind him far,*
> *And at the end two stingers:*
> *Both deadly sharp—sharper than steel, by far.*
> *His deep devouring jaws*
> *Gaped wide, like the grisly mouth of hell,*

And in either jaw were three rows of iron teeth
In which, still trickling blood and raw guts,
Recently devoured bodies did appear.

THE GOOD SIDE OF DRAGONS

But dragons are not always enemies of humans. Especially in Asia, the dragon is benevolent—though sometimes bossy. Most important, it is a symbol of leadership.

The Asian calendar is divided into twelve-year cycles, with each of those years associated with a particular animal. People born in the Year of the Dragon are said to be the best leaders, combining a strong will with a generous nature.

WHAT'S INSIDE A DRAGON'S BRAIN?

Some authorities say a magical gemstone, called draconite, can be found inside a dragon's head: "There is cut out of the dragon's brain a stone, but it is not a stone unless it be taken while the dragon is alive. For if the dragon dies first, the hardness vanishes away with his life. Men of excellent courage and audacity search out the holes where the dragons lie. Then watching until they come forth to feed, and passing by them with as much speed as they can, they cast them herbs to provoke sleep. So when the dragons are fast asleep, the men cut the stones out of their

In the last half of the twentieth century, the years of the dragon in the Asian calendar were roughly equivalent to these years on the Western calendar: 1952, 1964, 1976, 1988, 2000.

heads, and getting the booty of their heady enterprise, enjoy the reward of their rashness. The kings of the East wear these although they are so hard that no man can devise to imprint or engrave anything in it. It has a pure natural whiteness."

In ancient legend, the blood of dragons was also magical. This fits with a fact noted on Dumbledore's *Famous Witches and Wizards* trading card, that one of his achievements was figuring out the twelve uses of dragon's blood.

See also:

Potter, Harry

Who Were the First British Wizards?

Druids

WIZARDS EXISTED IN BRITAIN LONG BEFORE Hogwarts was founded. Early wizards were known as Druids (as in Druidess Cliodna, who is depicted on a *Famous Witches and Wizards* trading card). The name comes from the Celtic for "knowing the oak tree." They were the scholarly class in Britain and Gaul (what is now France).

Druids acted as local priests, teachers, and judges. They also gathered annually in what is now the French city of Chartres to debate broader questions and settle controversies.

The Roman ruler Julius Caesar, who conquered Gaul and Britain and recorded what he learned of those lands, said the Druids "know much about the stars and celestial motions, and about the size of the earth and universe, and about the essential nature of things, and about the powers and authority of the immortal gods; and these things they teach to their pupils."

Druid training could last as long as twenty years. As Caesar suggests, it included instruction in poetry, astronomy, and philosophy, as well as religion.

The Druids worshiped several nature gods—they believed in a religious force that pervaded all living things. They also believed in immortality and reincarnation. Their rituals included animal and perhaps even human sacrifice. Caesar claimed they used twigs and branches to build huge frame sculptures in the shape of a man, then filled the inside of the sculptures with living people and set the sculptures ablaze. However, some scholars dispute this assertion, saying Caesar was unfairly biased against the Druids because they vigorously resisted his rule.

See also:

Wizards

If Dumbledore Is So Powerful, Shouldn't He Fight Voldemort?

O FFICIALLY, ALBUS DUMBLEDORE IS SIMPLY the headmaster of Hogwarts. But he is significantly more important in the magical world than such a role would imply. He is the only wizard, other than Harry, whom Voldemort fears—one of the few unafraid to speak of the fallen wizard by name. He had been first choice to lead the Ministry of Magic, but, preferring to remain at Hogwarts, he plays a behind-the-scenes role, advising Minister Cornelius Fudge.

Dumbledore

Quite tall and thin, his hair and beard fall below his waist. He has a prominent, hawk-like nose, on which rest glasses with half-moon lenses. His Chocolate Frog trading card notes he is "considered by many the greatest wizard of modern times," and he has the titles to prove it: Order of Merlin (First Class), Grand Sorcerer, Chief Warlock, Supreme Mugwump, International Confederation of Wizards.

A Classic Wizard

Dumbledore certainly is a wizard in the legendary mold. One might easily mistake him for Merlin or Obi-Wan Kenobi of *Star Wars*. Gandalf, the wizard of J. R. R. Tolkien's *Lord of the Rings* books, could be a twin brother: "[Gandalf's] long white hair, his sweeping silver beard, and his broad shoulders, made him look like some wise king of ancient legend. In his aged face under great snowy brows his dark eyes were set like coals that could leap suddenly to fire." That description sounds a lot like the scene in *Goblet* when Dumbledore realizes Barty Crouch Jr. has been disguised as Mad-Eye Moody: "There was cold fury in every line of the ancient face; a sense of power radiated from Dumbledore as though he were giving off burning heat."

Why Not Search for Voldemort?

Dumbledore, his trading card tells us, "is particularly famous for his defeat of the dark wizard Grindelwald in 1945." Since that was the same year that Britain and its allies defeated Hitler and other enemies of democracy in the Second World War, we can take it as a hint that Dumbledore and Grindelwald had quite a struggle. So Dumbledore must be an accomplished fighter.

Dumbledore's first name means "white" in Latin. That befits a wizard with well-earned gray hair. It also makes him the perfect opponent of the "Dark" Lord.

His last name comes from an old English word for bumble bee. J. K. Rowling says she liked the idea that this music-lover might absent-mindedly hum to himself.

Why then would he let Harry face Voldemort? Surely he is powerful enough to find the Dark Lord and finish him once and for all?

A CHILD'S EYES

If only it were that easy. Dumbledore, for all his accomplishments and wisdom, is only human.

We usually see him as Harry would: all-knowing and all-powerful. He is the perfect parent—especially important to Harry, with his own parents dead and Sirius Black on the run. To Harry, who knows only the version written in history books, Dumbledore's achievements seem too impressive to ever be matched. Meanwhile, Harry is full of doubts about his own abilities.

But of course Dumbledore is only human. What could one expect of a person who likes chamber music, tenpin bowling, and lemon drops? He must have had all the same doubts as Harry when he was young—maybe more. History books record only part of the story. (Trading cards even less!) We know he makes mistakes, like hiring Gilderoy Lockhart to teach Defense Against the Dark Arts. Had Dumbledore been all-knowing, he would have seen through Lockhart. But no one can be expected to know everything.

It's possible—even likely—that Dumbledore has a larger plan for the defeat of Voldemort. That design could very well call for a one-on-one duel between himself and the Dark Lord, as a prelude to a final conflict between Voldemort and Harry. In any case, he appears to know more secrets than he has divulged so far, and will reveal his intentions only on his own schedule. For instance, he has never explained how Voldemort knew it was so important to attack Harry, even though Harry was only a year old.

Whatever role Dumbledore plays, we can be sure that a crucial lesson for Harry on the road to becoming a mature wizard is to see him as human, flawed like everyone else despite being deservedly revered. Only then will Harry be able to see his own character and accomplishments as equally admirable.

See also:

Hogwarts

Potter, Harry

Voldemort

Why Would Durmstrang Students Travel by Ship?

DURMSTRANG IS ONE OF TWO WIZARDING schools in continental Europe. Its exact location is a well-kept secret, but it is probably somewhere in northeastern Europe, judging from the uniforms—on top of robes of "deep bloodred," the students wear coats of "shaggy, matted fur"—and from the Russian names of Headmaster Igor Karkaroff and students such as Poliakoff.

Durmstrang

"Storm and Stress"

The school's name is a play on the German phrase *Sturm und Drang* ("storm and stress"). That term describes a type of literature devoted to grandeur, spectacle, and rebellion. It was an important trend in German literature in the 19th century. The foremost writer of that movement was Johann Wolfgang von Goethe, whose most famous work, *Faust*, details a man's pact with the Devil—like the pact

Karkaroff, a former Death Eater, made with Voldemort.

Another artist of the movement, composer Richard Wagner, wrote many dark operas, one of them based on the famous story of a ghost ship, *The Flying Dutchman.* That ship was doomed to roam the oceans endlessly because its captain had angrily denounced God during a storm.

PUREBRED EVIL

Durmstrang is a very different school from Hogwarts. While Hogwarts students are taught only Defense Against the Dark Arts, students at Durmstrang are taught the Dark Arts themselves. (This is the influence of headmaster Karkaroff, a former Death Eater.) As well, Durmstrang "does not admit Mudbloods," according to Draco Malfoy, whose father admires the Durmstrang doctrines and considered sending Draco there. This devotion to a nasty and highly questionable notion of purity befits the school's name. The artists of the *Sturm und Drang* movement, and Wagner in particular, were favorites of the Nazi government in Germany just before and during the Second World War. The Nazis were obsessed with killing anyone who did not fit their definition of a pureblooded German.

Sturm und Drang composer Richard Wagner also wrote a series of operas about a wizard named Alberic, who, like Harry, had an invisibility cloak. See **Wizards— Alberic Grunnion**.

EAST VERSUS WEST?

The differences between Hogwarts and Durmstrang also reflect long-standing animosity between countries of Western and Eastern Europe. Hogwarts, under Dumbledore's leadership, is a good example of the democratic traditions of the West. Durmstrang is a more severe place, breeding wizards who can't be trusted—just as Eastern Europe has long been viewed by outsiders. Significantly, by the end of *Goblet*, both sides recognize that their enmity must be put aside to fight a common foe.

Where Does Magic Come From?

WHEN RON WEASLEY'S FAMILY WINS A trip to Egypt in *Azkaban*, Hermione admits, "I'm really jealous. The ancient Egyptian wizards were fascinating." She would probably agree with the many scholars who consider Egypt to be the origin of magical knowledge.

EGYPTIAN RELIGION AND MAGIC

Hieroglyphs, the pictures ancient Egyptians used for a written language, record that Egyptian magic and religion were closely linked. The Egyptian gods, unlike those in other cultures, entrusted humankind with magical wisdom. (By comparison, according to Greek mythology the hero Prometheus—whose name means "to think ahead"—had to trick the gods into giving up fire, which represents life and knowledge.)

According to Egyptian religion, magic was created in the form of the god Heka soon

after the creation of the world. Heka's name actually became the word that meant "magic." After that word was passed into Greek, where it was given a local spelling and pronunciation, it became the word *mageia*, which gives us the English word we use today.

Another Egyptian god, Thoth, was even more closely associated with magic. He ruled the healing arts—always linked with wizardry in ancient cultures—as well as astronomy and mathematics. He was often pictured carrying a pen, and was said to have written secret books that revealed the mysteries of alchemy and science. One of these books was supposedly sealed within a golden box that was kept within a hidden temple.

The Egyptian god **Thoth** recorded his magical knowledge in books.

EGYPTIAN SPELLS

Egyptians relied heavily on charms and spells. Speaking of action was said to make it so. Sometimes those words were spoken over a wax or clay figurine that represented the person or thing to which the magic was directed. These spells were commonly used for healing, but less benevolent uses were known. One wizard, Weba-aner, was said to have transfigured a small figurine of a crocodile into a live animal at court. The deadly beast killed the lover of the adulterous queen, then was returned to its original form by the wizard. Another wizard-priest became a ruler by using this technique to "rule all kings by his magical power." He sank figures of his enemies' fleets, causing the actual ships to sink.

However, Egyptian magic was less concerned with earthly riches than with holiness. According to one text, "He who is a priest of the living . . . performs right actions without seeking a reward for them. Such a teacher lives a life of true piety."

The Egyptian god **Osiris** judged the dead.

SCARABS

Egypt is also the origin of the scarab, a beetle that Hogwarts students know from Potions class.

Scarabs are called dung beetles because

they gather and roll balls of dung in which they lay their eggs. In ancient Egypt this ball-rolling was seen to symbolize the movement of the sun. The scarab god Khepera was said to push the sun across the sky.

Eventually scarabs also came to symbolize immortality. Carved scarab amulets were placed on the heart of mummies to prepare them for their journey into the afterlife. Scarabs are still a common motif for jewelry.

See also:

Black, Sirius

Fawkes

An Egyptian drawing of a **scarab** beetle (with wings added) pushing a ball representing the sun.

Which Character Can't Die?

WHEN HARRY'S ADVENTURES BEGIN IN *Stone*, the oldest characters are Nicolas and Perenelle Flamel, who are both more than 600 years old. But they lose their immortality when the Sorcerer's Stone is lost. However, another important character may be truly immortal: Fawkes, Dumbledore's pet phoenix.

Fawkes

The phoenix is a magical, eternal bird. It lives for centuries—some people say five hundred years. The Latin poet Ovid asked:

> *How many creatures walking on this earth*
> *Have their first being in another form?*
> *Yet one exists that is itself forever,*
> *Reborn in ageless likeness through the years.*
> *It is that bird Assyrians call the Phoenix,*
> *Nor does he eat the common seeds and grasses,*
> *But drinks the juice of rare, sweet-burning*
> *   herbs.*
> *When he has done five hundred years of living*
> *He winds his nest high up a swaying palm*
> *And delicate dainty claws prepare his bed*
> *Of bark and spices, myrrh and cinnamon*
> *And dies while incense lifts his soul away.*

Then from his breast—or so the legend runs—
A little Phoenix rises over him,
To live, they say, the next five hundred years.

This sacred creature, almost always described as red and gold, was known as *benu* in ancient Egypt, where it originated. It was an important symbol of the city of Heliopolis ("Sun City"). In the Egyptian *Book of the Dead*, a religious text written about 2000 B.C., the phoenix claims, "I am the keeper of the volume of the book of things which are and of things which shall be."

In Egyptian hieroglyphics, the phoenix image conveys the passage of time, and it remains a symbol of immortality today. Writers often use the phoenix as a symbol of undying love and loyalty. In "The Canonization," the seventeenth-century poet John Donne writes to his wife,

"When the bird of wonder dies, the maiden phoenix, Her ashes new create another heir, As great in admiration as herself. . . ." William Shakespeare, *Henry VIII* (act V, scene ii).

The phoenix riddle hath more wit
By us; we two being one, are it.
So, to one neutral thing both sexes fit,
We die and rise the same, and prove
Mysterious by this love.

FAWKES'S NAME

Fawkes's name is related to the phoenix legend—but with a historical twist. Obviously he is named for Guy Fawkes, leader of a famous attempt to blow up the English Parliament building on November 5, 1605. The Gunpowder Plot, as it is called, was to be the start of a revolt by English Catholics, who were being persecuted at the time. The conspirators hid 36 barrels of gunpowder under the House of Lords, but there were so many conspirators that the plan leaked to authorities, who arrested the men and executed many of them. (The situation for Catholics only became worse.) In Britain, November 5 is now Guy Fawkes Day, celebrated with bonfires—like the funeral pyre of a phoenix.

See also:
Black, Sirius
Egypt

Was the Real Flamel a Successful Alchemist?

NICOLAS FLAMEL, AS MANY HARRY POTTER fans know, was an actual historical figure. Born near Paris about 1330, he tried several careers—poet, painter, and public scribe—before pursuing an interest in astrology. Then in 1357, according to his account, he was visited in a dream by an angel who showed him a book and said, "Flamel, look at this book. You will not in the least understand it, neither will anyone else; but the day will come when you will see in it something that no one else will see." The next day he saw that same volume in a bookseller's stall, offered for a cheap price because no one could understand its writing. With great effort, and the help of a scholar who could read Hebrew, Flamel deciphered the text, which seemed to be a manual for transmuting base metals into gold.

Unfortunately, the instructions called for a special ingredient—a philosopher's stone—without describing it specifically. Flamel

Flamel

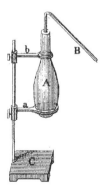

experimented for decades to find the mysterious substance. On January 17, 1383, as he related in his memoir:

> Finally I found the object of my search, and I knew it by its strong smell; and with it I accomplished the magic. I had learned the preparation of the first agent and had only to follow my book word by word. The first time I carried out the operation, I worked with quicksilver and transmuted about one and a half pounds of it into pure silver, better than silver from a mine. I put the results to the test several times. Later I accomplished the operation with the red stone on a similar amount of quicksilver on the 25th day of April of the same year when I transmuted the quicksilver into about the same amount of gold.
>
> This gold was clearly superior to ordinary gold. I accomplished the magic three times with [my wife] Perenelle's help.

This description—"its strong smell"—led other alchemists to believe the philosopher's stone was sulfur. But no one is known to have repeated the process.

According to history, Flamel died in 1410,

a few years after his wife, Perenelle. However, some of his followers believed that in addition to creating gold Flamel produced the Elixir of Life, which offers immortality. They said he and his wife actually lived on, sustained by the elixir.

In Harry's world, the faithful were proven correct. At the beginning of *Stone*, Flamel and his wife are both alive and well, despite being just shy of 660 years old. Unfortunately, when the stone is destroyed their elixir can no longer be produced, so they pass away.

See also:

Alchemy

Mirrors

Wizards

Why Would Fluffy Come From "a Greek Chappie"?

Fluffy

FLUFFY IS HAGRID'S PET DOG, GUARDIAN OF Nicolas Flamel's magic stone after it is removed from Gringotts Bank: "A monstrous dog, a dog that filled the whole space between ceiling and floor. It had three heads; three pairs of rolling, mad eyes; three noses, twitching and quivering in their direction; three drooling mouths."

Hagrid bought Fluffy from "a Greek chappie I met in the pub." That makes sense, because Fluffy is actually a magical creature from Greek mythology known as Cerberus. He was a sentry there, too. He guarded Hades, the underworld, where the souls of the dead go to live for eternity. It was his job to keep all living beings away, and to eat anyone trying to escape.

CERBERUS AND HERCULES

Cerberus plays a role in a famous Greek myth, the story of the twelve labors of Hercules. The hero Hercules had been tricked by the goddess

Hera into committing horrendous crimes, and was punished by becoming a servant to an unworthy king for twelve years. The king demanded that Hercules complete twelve tasks considered impossible. Most of them involved killing or capturing vicious beasts, like the Hydra, a creature with many heads. The last, considered the most difficult, was to capture Cerberus from his post at the gates of Hades and parade him before the king. Amazingly, Hercules did so, using just brute strength.

See also:
Centaurs
Sphinx

CERBERUS AND MUSIC

One other person got the better of Cerberus, but it wasn't with muscle. Orpheus, a gifted musician, braved the Underworld to rescue his beloved, Eurydice. Lacking the strength of Hercules, he played his lyre to tame Cerberus. It worked. He was able to sneak by the creature and escort Eurydice away. That's why the Greek chappie told Hagrid that music tames Fluffy.

Cerberus, from an illustration drawn about 1500.

Why Would the Forest Near Hogwarts Be "Forbidden"?

Forest

FORESTS ARE A FAVORITE CREATION OF writers, and J. K. Rowling's Forbidden Forest near Hogwarts has all the qualities one could expect. It is nature run wild, making it the opposite of civilized places like Hogwarts or the village of Hogsmeade. Within it live magical creatures older than humankind, like the unicorn. As well, just as there is knowledge in nature that humans have always tried

to understand—such as the wisdom of the nature gods worshiped by the Druids—the Forbidden Forest near Hogwarts is a place where secrets are kept and mysteries can be unraveled. Voldemort's murder of a unicorn in *Stone* reveals his presence to Harry; in *Chamber*, Harry and Ron follow spiders into the Forest and meet Aragog, who tells them a little about the monster in Hogwarts.

As with other forests in literature, Rowling's Forbidden Forest is also a dangerous place where one can lose one's way or one's sense of self. But forests can also offer refuge, and are home to spirits with a special knowledge of nature and healing. Hagrid, for instance, does not fear the Forbidden Forest. And if Harry ever needed to escape Voldemort, he could easily find himself protected by the Forbidden Forest and its residents, rather than endangered by them.

See also:

Centaurs

Druids

Hogwarts

Unicorns

Are All Giants All Bad?

G IANTS ARE THOUGHT BY MOST HUMANS—
probably unfairly—to be as dangerous
and cruel as they are large. Whatever the
truth, they have a troublesome history.

Giants

EARLY GIANTS

The first giants were the Gigantes of ancient
Greek mythology, born when the blood of
Uranus (the Heavens) fell upon Gaea (Earth).
The Gigantes fought the gods of Mount
Olympus—Zeus, Hera, Apollo, and others.
The Olympian gods needed the help of the
hero Hercules to defeat them. The Gigantes
were buried underneath mountains that then
became volcanoes.

Another race of mythical Greek giants was
known as the Cyclops. These monsters, who
had only one eye, created the thunderbolts of
Zeus. In Homer's epic poem *The Odyssey*, the
hero Odysseus and his men encounter a
Cyclops and barely escape.

The **Cyclops** of
Greek myth.

Both these races of giants, like those that
followed, were said to be vicious cannibals.

BRITISH GIANTS

Among later giants, the legend of a pair named Gog and Magog spread throughout the world, changing a bit from place to place. In Britain the story survives in the form of two large statues in Guildhall in London, first erected in the 1400s and said to portray the last of a race of giants destroyed by the legendary founder of London. (The statues, public favorites, have been replaced twice: first after the Great Fire of 1666, then after an air raid during the Second World War.)

A slightly different British legend combines those giants into a single monster named Gogmagog, who lived near Cornwall. In that version, a brave soldier threw the giant off a cliff, which is still called Giant's Leap.

Another British giant of legend, Gargantua, became famous in the 1500s as the main character in comical adventures written by a Frenchman, François Rabelais. Gargantua was something like the gigantic American woodsman Paul Bunyan. He was so huge that a tennis court fit inside one of his teeth. It took the milk of 17,913 cows to quench his thirst. In some legends, he was employed by King Arthur, and was credited with defeating Gog and Magog.

In two early books of the Bible, Genesis and Ezekiel, **Magog** is the name of the place from which **Gog** comes. In a later book, Revelations, Magog is a second creature or force who joins Gog in trying to destroy the world.

GIANTS AND MAGIC

According to the early historian Geoffrey of Monmouth, Stonehenge, the mysterious circle of huge stones in southern England, originated with the giants of Ireland. As he records, Merlin had been asked for advice on building a war memorial. The wizard replied:

"If you want to grace the burial place of these men with some lasting monument, send for the Giants' Ring which is on Mount Killaraus in Ireland. In that place there is a stone construction which no man of this period could ever erect, unless he combined great skill and artistry. The stones are enormous and there is no one alive strong enough to move them. If they are placed in position round this site, in the way in which they are erected over there, they will stand for ever. . . .

"These stones are connected with certain secret religious rites and they have various properties which are medicinally important. Many years ago the Giants transported them from the remotest confines of Africa and set them up in Ireland at a time when they inhabited that country. Their plan was that, whenever they

In Shakespeare's *As You Like It,* Rosalind anxiously asks her friend Celia about a young man: "What said he? How looked he? Where went he? Did he ask for me? Where remains he? How parted with thee? And when shalt thou see him again? Answer me in one word." Celia snaps back, "You must borrow me **Gargantua's** mouth first; 'tis a word too great for any mouth of this age's size." (act III, scene ii)

felt ill, baths should be prepared at the foot of the stones; for they used to pour water over them and to run this water into baths in which their sick were cured. What is more, they mixed the water with herbal concoctions and so healed their wounds. There is not a single stone among them that hasn't some medicinal virtue."

As Geoffrey tells it, the king took Merlin's advice and had the stones transported to their present site.

A SECRET EVERYONE KNOWS

In Harry's world, most wizards are prejudiced against giants. Hagrid never told anyone his mother was the giantess Fridwulfa because he was worried about what they would think. For the same reason, the headmistress of Beauxbatons, Madame Olympe Maxime, is reluctant to admit she is also half-giant. But anyone with common sense would guess that secret from her name. Olympe refers to the original giants of Olympus, and *maxime* means "great" or "very large" in French.

Geoffrey of Monmouth, like most early historians, relied on stories he was told, so his history of Britain mixes legends with actual events.

Which Real-Life Creature Still Eludes Scientists?

IN THE LAKE AT HOGWARTS LIVES A REAL-LIFE creature that is as mysterious as any magical beast. It is not elusive because it is small; in fact, it is the largest invertebrate on earth. It is the giant squid, which lives in waters so deep and far from shore that no human living today has seen one alive.

Giant Squid

Architeuthis, as scientists call it, can grow to 70 feet long. Its eyes, the largest of any animal, are well-suited for gathering what little light exists in the mile-deep waters of its home. There is no sunlight at those depths, but certain creatures have chemicals in their bodies that glow.

The French science fiction author Jules Verne wrote about the giant squid in his novel *20,000 Leagues Under the Sea*. The creature attacks the electric submarine in the story, *Nautilus*:

Before my eyes was a horrible monster,

worthy to figure in the legends of the marvelous. It was an immense cuttlefish, being eight yards long. It swam crossways in the direction of the *Nautilus* with great speed, watching us with its enormous staring green eyes. Its eight arms, or rather feet, fixed to its head, that have given the name of cephalopod to these animals, were twice as long as its body, and were twisted like the Furies' hair. One could see the 250 air-holes on the inner side of the tentacles. The monster's mouth, a horned beak like a parrot's, opened and shut vertically. Its tongue, a horned substance, furnished with several rows of pointed teeth, came out quivering from this veritable pair of shears.

Verne was following a long tradition in making the giant squid out to be a villain. But, turning our expectations about monsters upside-down as usual, J. K. Rowling's giant squid is kind. When Dennis Creevey falls into the lake in *Goblet*, the squid rescues him, placing him back into the boat.

Why Are Harry and Cedric Like Knights of the Round Table?

BOTH HARRY AND CEDRIC FIND THE GOBLET of Fire at the center of the maze in the Third Task of the Triwizard Tournament. As well as proving them to be exceptional wizards, this feat links them to the legends of King Arthur and the Round Table.

Goblet of Fire

The Goblet of Fire is "a large roughly hewn wooden cup" that would be "entirely unremarkable had it not been full to the brim with dancing blue-white flames." There is, of course, another goblet that launched tournaments and even battles, and which was said to hold magic power: the Holy Grail. That is the cup from which Jesus Christ is said to have drunk at the Last Supper. Though sometimes depicted as a shining silver goblet, the Holy Grail, being the cup of a poor carpenter, would probably have been made of wood— like the Goblet of Fire.

The Grail, like the Goblet, was a magical object. To drink from it was to be miraculously healed. And like the Goblet, it could sense whether or not a knight was worthy.

According to legend, King Arthur, praying for a sign from heaven during a barren period in his reign, sees the Grail. (In the earliest stories the Grail was a large platter; over time it became a cup.) He and his knights then undertake quests to either capture it or at least understand its significance. It is found by Galahad, son of Lancelot, because his soul is completely pure—rather like the soul of Cedric Diggory, who finds the Goblet of Fire with Harry.

Although Galahad finds the Grail, most of the legends focus on a character named Perceval. Born into a peasant family, Perceval eventually proves his virtue and becomes a Knight of the Round Table. Whether Percy Weasley will show the qualities exhibited by his namesake remains to be seen.

See also:

Mazes

Potter, Harry

Why Are Goblins Such Good Bankers?

N OT NEARLY AS FRIENDLY AS ELVES, AND more clever than gnomes, the goblins of Harry's world have rebelled against wizards several times in the past. The truce between the two sides is uneasy, and the wizard world has not yet embraced goblins.

Goblins

THE GOOD, THE BAD, AND THE UGLY

The word *goblin* derives from the Greek *kobalos*, meaning "rogue." The same word produced the German *kobold* or *kobolt* and the French *gobelin*. As the word suggests, they tend not to haunt a single family or home, but rather are given to roam.

Sometimes goblins are portrayed as more industrious than evil—adept at mining and metalwork, for example. Their cousins, the hobgoblins, also tended to be more pranksters than malefactors. Puck, "that merry wanderer of the night" from Shakespeare's *A Midsummer Night's Dream* is the best example.

They have even been known to do good deeds. Long before he wrote *A Christmas Carol*, Charles Dickens wrote "The Story of the Goblins Who Stole a Sexton," a Christmas story in which goblins showed a man named Gabriel Grub—"an ill-conditioned, cross-grained, surly fellow; a morose and lonely man, who consorted with nobody but himself"—the error of his ways:

People used to rid themselves of **goblins** by spreading flax seeds on their kitchen floor. For some reason, the goblin was compelled to pick up all the seeds—a very boring task. The goblin would soon look for fun elsewhere.

Seated on an upright tombstone, close to him, was a strange, unearthly figure, whom Gabriel felt at once was no being of this world. His long, fantastic legs which might have reached the ground, were cocked up, and crossed after a quaint, fantastic fashion; his sinewy arms were bare; and his hands rested on his knees. On his short, round body, he wore a close covering, ornamented with small slashes; a short cloak dangled at his back; the collar was cut into curious peaks, which served the goblin in lieu of ruff or neckerchief; and his shoes curled up at his toes into long points. On his head, he wore a broad-brimmed sugar-loaf hat, garnished with a single feather. The hat was covered with white frost; and the goblin looked as if he had sat on the same tombstone very comfortably, for two or three hundred years. He was sitting perfectly still; his tongue was put out, as if in derision; and he was grinning at Gabriel Grub with such a grin as only a goblin could call up.

"I am afraid my friends want you, Gabriel," said the goblin, thrusting his tongue farther into his cheek than ever— and a most astonishing tongue it was— "I'm afraid my friends want you, Gabriel," said the goblin.

Like the ghosts in *A Christmas Carol* who show Scrooge the meaning of Christmas, the goblins show Gabriel that the world isn't as bad as it seems.

However, goblins are most often portrayed like those of Christina Rosetti's poem, "Goblin Market":

> *We must not look at goblin men,*
> *We must not buy their fruits:*
> *Who knows upon what soil they fed*
> *Their hungry thirsty roots? . . .*
> *Their offers should not charm us,*
> *Their evil gifts would harm us.*

In J. R. R. Tolkien's chronicles of Middle-earth, goblins are called Orcs. Tolkien scholar Robert Foster called them an "evil race." He says they "were bred in mockery of Elves, and, like Elves, they were fierce warriors and did not die naturally. However, in all else they were different. . . . They hated all things of beauty, and loved to kill and destroy."

J. K. Rowling's goblins seem to be somewhere between good and evil. That balance makes them perfect guardians for Gringotts Bank, a task that requires they be both trustworthy and ruthless.

See also:

Boggarts
Cornish Pixies
Trolls
Veela

Which of Draco's Sidekicks Is also Named for a Dragon?

Goyle

JUST AS DRACO'S NAME COMES FROM THE Latin word for dragon, "Gregory Goyle" echoes "gargoyle," the monster seen near the roofs of some buildings. Less well known is the source of that creature's name: the Gargouille, a serpent-like dragon from France.

The Gargouille lived in the Seine River. It spouted water with great force, overturning fishing boats and flooding the countryside. St. Romain, the archbishop of Rouen, used a convict as bait to lure the monster from the river, then made the sign of the cross to subdue the beast. He walked it to the city, where the residents slaughtered it.

See also:
Malfoy
Names

Eventually, craftsmen carved images of the creature on the waterspouts they built to direct rainwater away from the walls of buildings.

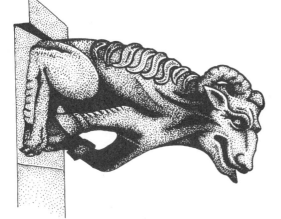

Which Creature Is Master of Both Earth and Sky?

HARRY'S HOUSE, GRYFFINDOR, LITERALLY means "golden griffin" in French. (*Or* is French for "gold.") It's an appropriate name for a house characterized by courage and virtue.

Griffins

Griffins are magical creatures, part lion, part eagle. They originated in India, where they guarded huge treasures of gold. In the third century A.D. a historian named Aelian wrote:

> I have heard that the Indian animal the Gryphon is a quadruped like a lion; that it has claws of enormous strength and that they resemble those of a lion. Men commonly report that it is winged and that the feathers along its back are black, and those on its front are red, while the actual wings are neither but are white. And Ctesias [an ancient Greek historian] records that its neck is variegated with

Griffin, from the seal of an Austrian town, about 1315.

feathers of a dark blue; that it has a beak like an eagle's, and a head too, just as artists portray it in pictures and sculpture. Its eyes, he says, are like fire.

It builds its lair among the mountains. Although it is not possible to capture the full-grown animal, hunters do take the young ones. Griffins engage too with other beasts and overcome them without difficulty, but they will not face the lion or the elephant.

THE MEANING OF GRIFFINS

Griffins have been part of literature and mythology for dozens of centuries. In that

time, their symbolic meaning has changed greatly. Scholar Hans Biedermann explains:

> A fabulous animal, symbolically significant for its domination of both the earth and the sky because of its lion's body and eagle's head and wings. In Greece the griffin was a symbol of vigilant strength; Apollo rode one, and griffins guarded the gold of Hyperborea [a mythical land of perpetual sunshine and happiness "beyond the north wind"]. The griffin was also an embodiment of Nemesis, the goddess of retribution, and turned her wheel of fortune. In legend the creature was a symbol of *superbia* (arrogant pride), because Alexander the Great was said to have tried to fly on the backs of griffins to the edge of the sky.
>
> At first also portrayed as a satanic figure entrapping human souls, the creature later became a symbol of the dual nature (divine and human) of Jesus Christ, precisely because of its mastery of earth and sky. The solar associations of both the lion and the eagle favored this positive reading. The griffin thus also became the adversary of serpents and

basilisks, both of which were seen as embodiments of satanic demons.

For the last thousand years, the griffin has been a favorite on family crests. An expert in heraldry says, "The griffin is very popular, for it has numerous virtues and apparently no vices. Notable among the former are vigilance, courage and strength." These are the very qualities embodied in the founder of Hogwarts whose name comes from this creature, Godric Gryffindor, and of the members of Gryffindor House.

See also:

Beasts

Hippogriffs

Why Do Parents Worry about Grindylows?

G RINDYLOWS ARE WATER DEMONS FROM
the legends of England's Yorkshire.
J. K. Rowling introduces them in *Azkaban*: "A
sickly green creature with sharp little horns
had its face pressed against the glass, pulling
faces and flexing its long, spindly fingers."

These dangerous creatures have a fondness
for ponds and lakes, where unsuspecting children who get too close to the water's edge can
be caught and dragged under the surface. In
Lancashire, the same demon is known as
Jenny Greenteeth. In other parts of England it
is known as Nellie Long-Arms. A relative of
the grindylow, Peg o' the Well, haunts wells.

Carol Rose, an expert on demons and spirits, calls grindylows "nursery bogies, described
with vigor by watchful nursemaids and anxious parents in order to prevent the untimely
death of children in such fearful places." But
when Harry dives into the Hogwarts lake to

Grindylows

See also:

Kappas

Giant Squid

Merpeople

rescue Ron during the second task of the Triwizard Tournament, the grindylows who grab his leg and robes feel very real to him.

Which Is the Least Likely Magical Creature?

BUCKBEAK THE HIPPOGRIFF, INTRODUCED IN *Azkaban*, is more than just an unusual magical creature. With the bird-like head and forelegs of a griffin attached to the body of a horse, hippogriffs are an especially odd combination. That's just what was intended by the man who imagined them, a sixteenth-century author with sense of humor.

Hippogriffs

The Roman poet Virgil once described something as impossible by saying it would happen when "griffins were mated with horses." The phrase stuck. For centuries it was used just as someone today might say, "When pigs have wings." Ludovico Ariosto, an Italian court poet of the early 1500s, remembered that line when he was writing *Orlando Furioso*, an epic story about the knights of Charlemagne, a king who ruled much of Europe in the ninth century. Deciding the time had come to make Virgil's unlikely match, he created the hippogriff. (The Greek word for horse is *hippos*.)

According to Ariosto, the hippogriff comes from the Rhiphaean Mountains, "far beyond the icebound seas." The creature appears in the story when Charlemagne's brave niece, Bradamante, searches for her beloved, a knight named Rogero. Bradamante discovers Rogero is the captive of an enchanter who rides the strange creature, which few people have seen before. After defeating the enchanter and freeing Rogero, Bradamante approaches the beast:

> They descended from the mountain to the spot where the encounter had taken place. There they found the Hippogriff, with the magic buckler in its wrapper, hanging to his saddle-bow. Bradamante advanced to seize the bridle; the Hippogriff seemed to wait her approach, but before she reached him he spread his wings and flew away to a neighboring hill, and in the same manner, a second time, eluded her efforts.
>
> Rogero and the other liberated knights dispersed over the plain and hilltops to secure him, and at last the animal allowed Rogero to seize his rein. The fearless Rogero hesitated not to vault upon

his back, and let him feel his spurs, which so roused his mettle that, after galloping a short distance, he suddenly spread his wings, and soared into the air.

Bradamante had the grief to see her lover snatched away from her at the very moment of reunion. Rogero, who knew not the art of directing the horse, was unable to control his flight. He found himself carried over the tops of the mountains, so far above them that he could hardly distinguish what was land and what water.

The Hippogriff directed his flight to the west, and cleaved the air as swiftly as a new-rigged vessel cut the waves,

impelled by the freshest and most favorable gales.

In another episode of the story, a different knight, Astolfo, rides the same hippogriff across the world:

> Hawk and eagle soar a course less free. Over the wide land of Gaul the warrior flew, from Pyrenees to Rhine, from sea to sea. To Aragon he passed out of Navarre, leaving people below wondering at the sight, then crossed Castile, Gallicia, Lisbon, Seville, and Cordova. He left no coast or inland plain of Spain unexplored.
>
> From the Atlantic to the further side of Egypt, bent over Africa, he turned. Morocco, Fez, and Oran, looking down, noble Biserta next and Tunis-town. Tripoli, Berniche, Ptolomitta he viewed, and into Asia's land the Nile he pursued.

See also:
Beasts
Griffins

Eventually Astolfo rides the hippogriff all the way to Paradise. Later, he respectfully sets it free. One can understand why J. K. Rowling says in *Beasts* that the hippogriff "is now found worldwide."

Why Would Anyone Go to School with a Slytherin?

THE WRITER PICO IYER, WHO ATTENDED two old British boarding schools—the Dragon School and Eton—says "much in the Harry Potter universe can seem familiar":

Hogwarts

Here are all the rites I remember as vividly as lemon drops: the cryptic list of instructions that would appear through the mail, describing what we must—and mustn't—bring to school (the point of all the rules being not to make order so much as to enforce obedience); the trip to dusty old shops with creaky family names—New & Lingwood or Alden & Blackwell—where aged men would fit us out with the approved uniform and equipment, as they had done for our fathers and our fathers' fathers; the special school train that would be waiting in a London station to transport us to our cells. Once the doors clanged shut behind us, we knew we were inside an alternative reality where none of the usual rules applied. . . .

It is fitting that Harry begins each school year with a ride on the **Hogwarts Express**. J. K. Rowling thought up the stories during a train ride.

One could even say that the stranger the detail in Rowling's world, the closer it is to something everyday to us as gruel. Harry plays Quidditch, a peculiar game featuring "Bludgers" and "Chasers" and "Quaffles"; we had three brutal sports not played in any other school, the most savage of which had "walls" and "behinds" and no official goal scored since 1909. At Harry's school, inscrutably, "the third-floor corridor on the right-hand side is out of bounds"; at Eton, we were not allowed to walk on one side of the main road through town (for reasons that were not forthcoming). As for ghosts, we ate and slept and studied around busts and portraits and the scribbled desktop signatures of [the British prime ministers] Gladstone, Wellington and Pitt the Elder.

But some people say that Hogwarts is quite different from most boarding schools. It is pleasant: the food is delicious, and Harry sleeps in a four-poster bed. It is lenient: though disobedience may cost a few house points, the teachers are very forgiving. Most of all, Dumbledore has made it a place of eminent fairness.

Given how agreeable the school can be, one has to wonder what the Slytherins are doing there. Every bit of trouble seems to start with a Slytherin. There doesn't seem to be a decent student in that house. Its philosophy seems to be the same dark thought expressed by Quirrell in *Chamber*: "There is no good and evil, there is only power, and those too weak to seek it." Salazar Slytherin, the Hogwarts founder for which the house was named, was so devious he even built the Chamber of Secrets under the school without telling the other founders. So wouldn't it make sense to just get rid of them?

Actually, that would seem to be the opposite of J. K. Rowling's philosophy. In fact, the presence of Slytherins at Hogwarts seems to say a lot about her ideas of good and evil.

Within the walls of Hogwarts, Dumbledore's leadership has created an appealing ideal. Evil is not pushed away fearfully; or simply met with courageous force. It is to be countered with compassion. More than once, Dumbledore has demonstrated a strong faith that fallen wizards can redeem themselves.

Each of the four founders of Hogwarts had individual qualities that form part of a balanced whole. Even Slytherin's ambition can be directed toward good—provided it is balanced with the characteristics displayed by the others. It is part of reality, part of every individual—just as Harry has a bit of Voldemort in him. Trying to eliminate it would be silly, as well as impossible.

See also:

Durmstrang

Which Creature May Not Bow Its Head?

I N *AZKABAN*, HARRY LEARNS ABOUT KAPPAS, "creepy, water-dwellers that looked like scaly monkeys." They are mentioned again in *Beasts*.

Kappas

J. K. Rowling did not invent kappas. They are, as she says in *Beasts*, water demons of Japanese legend. (In *Azkaban*, Professor Snape makes an error when he informs Harry's class that "the kappa is more commonly found in Mongolia.") Like the grindylows who live near Hogwarts, kappas live in lakes and rivers, and capture people in the water. They are also known as Kawako, which means "Child of the River."

The description in *Beasts*, odd as it sounds, is true to legend. Kappas can be vicious and enjoy the taste of blood. However, a human may escape from a kappa by exploiting the creature's greatest weakness. Its vitality is drawn from a saucer-like depression on its head, which must remain filled with water. If

See also:

Beasts

Grindylows

Merpeople

one offers a polite and ceremonious bow, the kappa will be obligated to return it. The water will spill and the kappa will be defeated. As well, for some long-forgotten reason, kappas love cucumbers almost as they love human blood. A gift of a cucumber may win the friendship of a kappa, who might then reveal secrets about medicine.

What Is the Most Important Language for Wizards?

U NLIKE MANY SCHOOLS, HOGWARTS DOES not seem to emphasize learning foreign languages, at least not in its first few years. But there is one language that even first-year students encounter often: Latin. Many charms, spells, and curses are simply Latin words for the desired effect. For instance, "Lumos," the spell that causes a light to appear at the end of a wizard's wand, is a Latin word meaning "light." "Nox," the spell that extinguishes the wand's light, is the Latin word for "darkness."

Latin is used in other places, also. For example, Mad-Eye Moody was once an Auror, a sort of police officer whose job is to bring bad wizards to justice. In Latin, *aurora* is another word for "light," so Auror is the perfect name for someone who fights darkness. As well, the Hogwarts motto is Latin: *Drago dormiens nunquam titillandus* ("Never tickle a

Latin

Historians say the oldest example of Latin is four words engraved on a cloak pin from the 6th or 7th century B.C. They named the owner of the cloak.

Do not try this at home!:

The Ministry says three curses are "unforgivable," punishable by a life sentence at Azkaban for any wizard who performs them on another human. They are "Crucio," which causes extreme pain (the Latin *crucio* means to torture or torment); "Imperio," which puts the subject under the wizard's complete control (the Latin *impero* means to order or command) and "Avada Kedavra," the Killing Curse (see **Avada Kedavra**).

sleeping dragon"). J. K. Rowling herself has said, "I like to think that the wizards use this dead language as a living language."

It makes sense that Latin would be so important. After the Romans conquered Europe (including Britain) about two thousand years ago, Latin became a common language, one that could be used anywhere in the empire. Scholars relied on it to ensure that their work could be shared. It was the also the primary language of Christianity. And for centuries, most books were written in Latin, because every educated person could be expected to know it.

LATIN FOR WIZARDS

Here are a few spells that come from Latin:

Accio: Summoning charm. From the Latin *accio*, to call or summon.

Aparecium: Makes invisible ink appear. From *appareo*, to become visible or appear.

Conjunctivitus Curse: Impairs eyesight. From *coniugo*, to bind together. Eyes have connective tissue called the conjunctiva. When this gets infected, a person gets conjunctivitis, commonly called "pink eye."

Deletrius: Makes things disappear. From *deleo*, to erase or destroy.

Densaugeo: Makes something grow uncontrollably. Perhaps from *denso*, to thicken. (Draco Malfoy directs this curse to Harry, but it ricochets and instead hits Hermione in the teeth.)

Diffindo: Splits things. From *diffindo*, to split or break apart.

Dissendium: Opens things, such as the statue of the witch that guards the secret passage from Hogwarts to Honeydukes. From *dissiedo*, to be separated.

Many English words—estimates vary from 30 to 60 percent—have Latin roots.

Enervate: Invigorates things. (Oddly, this spell has an effect that is exactly the opposite of its meaning in both Latin and English. In English, "enervate" means to weaken; and its Latin root, *enervo*, means the same. Neither means energize.)

Expecto Patronum: Produces a patronus (a guardian). From *expecto*, to throw out; and *patronus*, guardian.

As a general rule of magic, successfully performing a spell requires more than just saying a few words. How the spell is spoken—for instance, how confidently—can have great consequence. Casting a spell can require an enormous amount of energy, so a wizard's power is an important factor.

Expelliarmus: Disarms an opponent. From the Latin *expello*, to drive out or expel; and *arma*, weapon.

Fidelius Charm: Places a secret in another trusted person. From *fidelus*, faithful, trusted, trustworthy.

Finite Incantatem: Ends others spells. From *finite*, end; and *incantantem*, incantation or spell.

Impedimenta: Stops a person or thing. From *impedimentum*, impediment, hindrance.

Incendio: Used to travel by Floo from fireplace to fireplace. From *incendia,* fire.

Obliviate: Makes a person forget. From *oblivio*, oblivion, forgetfulness.

Petrificus Totalus: Immobilizes a person. From *petra*, rock.

Prior Incantatem: Reveals the previous spell cast by a wand. From *prior*, prior or previous; and *incantatem*, incantation or spell.

Rictusempra: Tickles. From *rictus*, a laughing smile.

Riddikulus: Makes something seem funny. Used to dispel a boggart. From *ridiculus*, laughable.

Ruparo: Repairs things. From *reparare*, repair.

Wingardium Leviosa. Can make something fly. From *levis*: light (which gives us the English word "levitate").

In Latin, the letter "v" is pronounced like "w." So *levis* would be pronounced as "le-wis."

LATIN FOR EVERYONE

Though most spells and curses are just single words, Latin can be used as an everyday language. In fact, it is still the official language of the Vatican. In an amusing book titled *Latin for All Occasions*, author Henry Beard offers a few expressions one might find useful:

What's happening?
Quid fit?

My dog ate it.
Canis meus id comedit.

It was that way when I got here.
Ita erat quando hic adveni.

Your fly is open.
Braccae tuae aperiuntur.

Rad, dude!
Radicitus, comes!

No way.
Nullo modo.

Fat chance.
Fors fortis.

Read my lips.
Labra lege.

Accidentally on purpose.
Casu consulto.

In addition, Beard offers this bumper sticker:
SI HOC ADFIXUM IN OBICE LEGERE POTES, ET LIBERALITER EDUCATUS ET NIMIS PROPINQUUS ADES. It means: "If you can read this bumper sticker, you are both very well educated and much too close."

See also:
Malfoy
Names

Why Is Each Malfoy Aptly Named?

J. K. ROWLING MUST HAVE HAD FUN CHOOSING names for the villainous Malfoys. Each one is loaded with meaning and history.

The family name derives from the Latin *maleficus,* meaning evil-doer. In medieval times the word was used to describe witches, whose evil acts were called maleficia. Witchcraft scholar Rosemary Ellen Guiley writes: "In its narrowest definition, *maleficia* meant damage to crops and illness or death to animals. In its broadest, it included anything with a negative impact upon a person: loss of love, storms, insanity, disease, bad luck, financial problems, lice infestations, even death. If a villager muttered a threat or a wish for calamity upon someone and misfortune of any sort occurred to the victim—*maleficia.* If the local wise woman administered a remedy for an illness and the patient worsened or died—*maleficia.* If a hail storm destroyed the crop, the cows wouldn't give milk or the horse

Malfoy

In 1484, the authors of *Malleus Maleficarum* were instructed by Pope Innocent VIII to prosecute witches in Germany.

went lame—*maleficia.*" One of the first books on witchcraft and sorcery, the most significant of its time, was titled *Malleus Maleficarum* ("The Witch's Hammer"). Published in 1486, it was written by two witch hunters to help others catch witches. For two hundred years it was the most popular book after the Bible. The Latin word has been preserved in many languages. For instance, *maleficent* in English is defined as harmful or evil in intent or effect. *Mal foi* is French for "bad faith."

Draco has a double meaning in Latin, both "dragon" and "snake." (Many languages used the same word for both.) Not surprisingly, Draco Malfoy is a Slytherin.

Draco's father is Lucius Malfoy—an echo of "Lucifer," which has come to be a name for the Devil. That fits Lucius, a powerful Death Eater.

Draco's mother is Narcissa. Her name comes from Greek myth. The story goes that a handsome young man named Narcissus was very vain, so he was cursed by a god to fall in love with himself. Narcissus fell into a river while admiring his own reflection and drowned.

See also:

Goyle

Names

Why Won't Wizards Go Near a Manticore?

Manticores

IN *AZKABAN*, WHILE TRYING TO FIND A LEGAL precedent that might save Buckbeak the hippogriff, Hermione comes across a revealing reference: "This might help, look—a manticore savaged someone in 1296, and they let the manticore off—oh—no, that was only because everyone was too scared to go near it."

That's not surprising. The manticore may be the nastiest magical creature. It is a combination of man and beast, with sharp teeth and a vicious manner. Its name comes from the old Persian *martikhora*, meaning "man-eater."

It seems to have lived throughout ancient Asia. A frightening description was sketched in the second century by a Roman historian who drew from reports written as much as seven hundred years earlier:

There is in India a wild beast, powerful, daring, as big as the largest lion, of a red color like cinnabar, shaggy like a dog, and in the language of India it is called Marti-choras. Its face however is not that of a wild beast but of a man, and it has three rows of teeth set in its upper jaw and three in the lower; these are exceedingly sharp and larger than the fangs of a hound. Its ears also resemble a man's, except that they are larger and shaggy; its eyes are blue-grey and they too are like a man's, but its feet and claws, you must know, are those of a lion.

To the end of its tail is attached the sting of a scorpion, and this might be over a cubit [eighteen inches] in length; and the tail has stings at intervals on either side. But the tip of the tail gives a fatal sting to anyone who encounters it, and death is immediate.

Manticore, from a 1607 woodcut.

If one pursues the beast it lets fly its stings, like arrows, sideways, and it can shoot a great distance; and when it discharges its stings straight ahead it bends its tail back; if however it shoots in a backward direction, then it stretches its tail to its full extent. Any creature that the missile hits it kills; the elephant alone it does not kill. These stings which it shoots are a foot long and thickness of a bulrush. One writer asserts (and he says that the Indians confirm his words) that in the places where those stings have been let fly others spring up, so that this evil produces a crop.

According to the same writer the Manticore devours human beings; indeed it will slaughter a great number; and it lies in wait not for a single man but would set upon two or even three men, and alone overcomes even that number.

The Indians hunt the young of these animals while they are still without stings in their tails, which they then crush with a stone to prevent them from growing stings. The sound of their voice is as near as possible that of a trumpet.

Carol Rose, an expert in magical creatures, says in the Middle Ages the manticore was thought to be a representative of the prophet **Jeremiah**. This connection derived from the belief that the manticore lived deep in the Earth. Jeremiah had been imprisoned in a dungeon.

A more recent description comes from the

famous French poet and novelist of the nineteenth century, Gustave Flaubert. In *The
Temptation of Saint Anthony*, Flaubert's manticore makes this colorful announcement: "The
iridescence of my scarlet hide blends into the
shimmering brightness of the desert sands.
Through my nostrils I exhale the horror of
the lonely places of the earth. I spit out pesti-
lence. I consume armies when they venture
into the desert. My nails are twisted into
talons, like drills, my teeth are cut like those
of a saw; my restless tail prickles with darts,
which I shoot left and right, before me,
behind. Watch!"

See also:
Beasts

Why Is the Third Task Set in a Maze?

THE THIRD AND FINAL TASK OF THE Triwizard Tournament is set within a maze built just for that purpose. Within it the competitors encounter a boggart, a sphinx, a Blast-Ended Skrewt, a giant spider, and a golden mist that turns them upside down. At the center is the Goblet of Fire.

Mazes

THE LABYRINTH OF CRETE

The maze—or labyrinth—is central to one of the best-known Greek myths about a hero's test of skill, the story of Theseus and the Minotaur. That labyrinth was built on the island of Crete by Daedalus, perhaps the most able inventor of his time. It was created to hold the pet of King Minos—a man-eating monster with a bull's body and a human head, known as the Minotaur.

At the time, Crete dominated Athens, which was forced to pay an annual tribute of seven young men and seven young women to

The **Minotaur**, from a vase of the 5th century B.C.

Crete. Every year these unlucky souls were sent into the labyrinth, which was too confusing to escape, and were eaten by the Minotaur. One year Theseus, son of the Athenian king, was among the offerings. But Minos's daughter Ariadne fell in love with him before he entered the labyrinth. To save his life, she gave him a sword to kill the Minotaur and a ball of thread to trail behind him so he could find his way back.

Although Theseus proved ungrateful to Ariadne, after his success in the labyrinth he became one of the greatest kings of Athens.

See also:

Centaurs

Fluffy

Why Might Prof. McGonagall Appear as a Cat?

T HE VERY FIRST WIZARD TO APPEAR IN *Stone* (even before Harry), is Minerva McGonagall, who lurks at Number Four Privet Drive in the form of a tabby cat. (A cat reading a map, actually—quite a shock to Mr. Dursley, who isn't entirely sure if such a thing is possible or if, instead, it is "a trick of the light.")

Though Prof. McGonagall may become a cat because it best reflects her personality, a cat would be an appropriate choice for many witches and wizards. Cats are not only ancient civilized pets—domesticated for perhaps five thousand years—they have long been linked with magic. Being nocturnal, they naturally came to be associated with darkness, the moon, and the spirit world.

McGonagall

The Egyptian cat-goddess, **Bast**

ANCIENT CATS

Cats were revered in the ancient cultures of Egypt and India, where mysticism originated. The city of Bubasti, at one time the capital of

Egypt, was devoted to the worship of the cat-headed goddess, Bast. Hundreds of thousands of pilgrims flocked to the city each year. Cats were given elaborate funerals.

Sacred rituals also honored cats in Europe. In ancient Rome, the goddess Diana had the power to transform herself into a cat. In Scandinavia, Freya, the Norse goddess of love, marriage, and fertility, was said to travel in a chariot drawn by two cats. Cats were also honored in early British history. But as Christianity replaced paganism, cats became objects of scorn, fear, and superstition.

See also:

Animagus

Black, Sirius

When Mr. Dursley stares at the tabby form of McGonagall, and she stares back, it's no surprise that Dursley senses (though only for a moment until his attention wanders!) an omen.

Why Might a Human Fear Merpeople?

F ROM THE LATIN WORD *MARE*, MEANING "sea," comes the name of these creatures known all over the world. The merpeople who live in the lake at Hogwarts, like so many others in literature, have green skin and long green hair. They have human torsos but silver fish tails instead of legs. (J. K. Rowling also adds some details that make her merpeople unique. Their houses are arranged in villages like those in the suburbs on land, and they make pets of grindylows.)

Legends of merpeople exist in nearly every culture. For instance, it was once said that the French aristocracy descended from a mermaid named Melusina.

As Rowling says in *Beasts*, the Sirens of Greek mythology are similar to mermaids. They

Merpeople

sing to the sailors of ships that pass by, enchanting them to their deaths on nearby rocks.

When Harry meets the merpeople during the second task of the Triwizard Tournament, he finds the same danger that contact with merpeople often symbolizes: the risk that the sea will prove so alluring that one will never return to land. As a character in one of the "Twice-Told Tales" of the early American author Nathaniel Hawthorne tells a young woman, "I fancied you akin to the race of mermaids, and thought how pleasant it would be to dwell with you among the quiet coves, in the shadows of the cliffs, and to roam along secluded beaches of the purest sand, and when our northern shores grew bleak, to haunt the islands, green and lonely, far amid summer seas."

See also:

Beasts

Grindylows

Kappas

Why Are Mirrors Magical?

F OR THOUSANDS OF YEARS, THE FOLKLORE
of wizards has mentioned mirrors. Being
expensive to make in ancient times, mirrors
were quite rare and had the power to inspire
surprise and awe. According to some legends
they were tools of the Devil, used for capturing souls just as they captured images. In the
Middle Ages wizards stared into mirrors to
divine the future or answer great questions.
This was called "scrying."

Mirrors

The most famous magical mirror in literature is certainly the one belonging to the evil
queen in Snow White. There are many others
as well. In a tale from the *Arabian Nights*, a
genie gave Prince Alasnam a mirror that
would reveal whether or not a lover could be
trusted. In a poem from Elizabethan England,
The Faerie Queen, Merlin created a mirror for
King Ryence with similar powers:

> *The great Magician Merlin had devised,*
> *By his deep science, and hell-dreaded might,*
> *A looking-glass, right wondrously built.*
> *This mirror showed in perfect sight,*

Witchcraft scholar Rosemary Ellen Guiley found instructions for making a magic mirror in the writings of medieval wizard Albert Magnus: "Buy a looking glass and inscribe upon it 'S. Solam S. Tattler S. Echogordner Gematur.' Bury it at a crossroads during an uneven hour. On the third day, go to the spot at the same hour and dig it up—but do not be the first person to gaze into the mirror. It is best to let a dog or a cat take the first look."

Whatever thing was in the world,
That the looker hoped to find;
Whatever foe had done, or friend or fiend,
Was thus discovered therein.

This mirror is very much like the one described by another famous British poet who lived three hundred years before Spenser. Geoffrey Chaucer—one of the first poets to write in English—created a long series of stories called *The Canterbury Tales*, each of which is narrated by a different fictional character making a pilgrimage to a shrine at Canterbury, England. In one of the stories, "The Squire's Tale," a mirror is given to a king named Cambinskan from the King of Araby and Ind:

This mirror,
Has power such that in it men may see
When there shall happen any adversity
Unto your realm, and to yourself also;
And openly who is your friend or foe.
More than all this, if any lady bright
Has her heart set on any kind of knight
If he be false she shall his treason see.

MAGIC PORTALS

As well as tools for divination, mirrors are

often portals to other worlds, like the one imagined by Lewis Carroll's Alice in *Through the Looking-glass*:

> "Now, if you'll only wait, Kitty, and not talk so much, I'll tell you all my ideas about Looking-glass House. First, there's the room you can see through the glass—that's just the same as our drawing room, only the things go the other way. . . . Let's pretend there's a way of getting through into it, somehow, Kitty. Let's pretend the glass has got all soft like gauze, so that we can get through. Why, it's turning into a sort of mist now, I declare! It'll be easy enough to get through—" She was up on the chimney-piece while she said this, though she hardly knew how she had got there. And certainly the glass was beginning to melt away, just like a bright mist.

THE MIRROR OF ERISED

Most of all, mirrors are a reflection of the self, for better or worse. That is why they can be so dangerous. The Mirror of Erised in *Stone* is certainly this sort of mirror. It stands "as high as the ceiling, with an ornate gold frame." At the top the following words are carved: "Erised stra ehru oyt ube cafru oyt on wohsi." Obviously, this message is the mirror image of "I show not your face but your heart's desire." And what could be better than that? Anything, apparently, as Ron tells Harry: "Dumbledore was right, that mirror could drive you mad."

Although the Mirror of Erised is "the key to finding the Stone," it is also a test of one's character. Vanity and selfishness, central to the act of looking in a mirror, are corrupt qualities. Because only someone with rare virtue deserves his desire, only someone who looks in the mirror and sees others (as when Harry sees his parents in it) or sees himself committing a selfless act (such as keeping the Stone from Voldemort) will receive what he wishes.

John Dee
(1527–1608), a favorite wizard of Britain's Queen Elizabeth I, often used a mirror for divination.

Which of Voldemort's Cohorts Comes from India?

I N *GOBLET*, VOLDEMORT IS KEPT ALIVE BY the poison of a large snake, Nagini. This is no ordinary snake. It has a royal bloodline and an important role in mythology.

Naga is Sanskrit for snake, and *nagi* the word for a female. (*Nag* is also the word for snake in several modern languages.) In Buddhism and Hinduism, Nagas are a race of semi-divine snakes with great powers. They live in a beautiful undergound city. Some have many heads. On the head of naga king Vasuki is a brilliant jewel, Nagamani, which has miraculous healing powers. In some legends the nagas are human from head to waist and serpent from the waist down. Female Nagas are known as Nagini.

A naga is said to have protected the Buddha, who was meditating under a tree during a great storm, by wrapping itself around him and spreading its heads to form an umbrella for him. As well, the world is said to rest on

Nagini

A **naga**, from a Sri Lankan stone carving.

the many heads of a naga named Ananta. And the naga king, Vasuki, was used by the gods to churn the ocean to create Amrita, an elixir of immortality. Not coincidentally, this is just what Voldemort seeks.

See also:

Basilisk

Nagas share an interesting connection with the basilisk. Just as roosters are the enemy of a basilisk, the constant foe of the Naga is Garuda, a powerful mythical bird.

Where Do Those Names Come From?!

DOES ANY WRITER CREATE NAMES WITH more care or a greater sense of humor than J. K. Rowling? She uses foreign words, puns, and anagrams; makes references to history and myth; and often takes names from maps. Occasionally she makes them up out of thin air, in the case of Quidditch. One clever fan noticed that the letters in the game's name relate to the names of its balls: *Qua*ffle, blu*d*ger, blu*d*ger, and sn*itch*. Even if Rowling didn't use the same reasoning, one can see why the name felt right to her.

She not only invents words, she invents fun histories for them. In *Quidditch Through the Ages,* written long after she introduced the game, she artfully answers the many queries of her fans by revealing that in Harry's world the game got its name from the place it was first played, Queerditch Marsh.

Often the names reveal something about

Names

the character's personality. Sometimes the references are so obscure one has to imagine Rowling is just enjoying a private joke. One thing is certain: Every name is worth a little digging for hidden meaning. Here are a few of them, with the references revealed.

Acronyms

O.W.L.s: Ordinary Wizarding Levels. To pass this test would prove one wise.

N.E.W.T.s: Nastily Exhausting Wizarding Tests: Newts are familiar from the brew mixed by the three witches at the beginning of Shakespeare's *Macbeth*: "Eye of newt and toe of frog, wool of bat and tongue of dog."

The **Potters** were named after one of J. K. Rowling's neighbors.

Geography

Bagshot, Bathilda (the author of *A History of Magic*): Bagshot is a town near London.

Dursley: A town near J. K. Rowling's birthplace.

Firenze: Italian name for the city of Florence.

Flitwick, Professor (Charms teacher): Flitwick is a town in England.

Snape, Severus: Snape is the name of another English village.

Foreign Words

Beauxbatons: French for "beautiful wands."

Delacour, Fleur: French for "flower of the court," as in a noblewoman.

Mosag: Gaelic for nasty, dirty woman.

Literature

Diggory, Cedric: Digory Kirke is a hero of some of J. K. Rowling's favorite books, *The Chronicles of Narnia* by C. S. Lewis. Notice that *Cedric* not far from a rearrangement of *Kirke*.

Flint, Marcus (captain of the Slytherin Quidditch team). Possibly named for Captain John Flint from Robert Louis Stevenson's *Treasure Island*. (Rudolf Hein, creator of a website devoted to Harry Potter names, made this clever connection.)

Lockhart, Gilderoy: The first name of this phony refers to his being gilded (covered in a thin gold foil) to make him seem intelligent and attractive. The last name

fits his role as a writer of wizard lore. A man named J. G. Lockhart was the son-in-law and biographer of Sir Walter Scott, the Scottish author whose skills earned him the nickname "Wizard of the North."

HISTORY

Elfric the Eager (an evil wizard): Elfric (also Aelfric) was a common name in Anglo-Saxon England. One Elfric was a notorious traitor, an army commander who feigned sickness on the eve of battle and warned the enemy army so it could escape.

Grey, Lady: Lady Jane Grey was the queen of England for nine days in 1553, before being deposed. She was only fourteen years old at the time. She was beheaded the next year.

Slytherin, Salazar: António de Oliveira Salazar was dictator of Portugal—where J. K. Rowling once lived—from 1932 to 1968. He was known for very harsh policies. (Another smart connection made by Rudolf Hein.)

RELIGION AND MYTHOLOGY

Hermes: Percy Weasley's owl. Hermes was the messenger of the Greek gods.

Lupin, Remus (a werewolf): *Lupus* is Latin for "wolf." The legendary founders of Rome, who as children were suckled by a wolf, were named Romulus and Remus.

Patil, Parvati: Parvati is a Hindu goddess.

SAINTS

Hedwig: A saint who lived in Germany in the twelfth and thirteenth centuries. An order of nuns established under her patronage chose as its work the education of orphaned children—like Harry.

Ronan (centaur): An Irish saint. (As some readers have pointed out, Ronan the centaur has red hair!)

MISCELLANEOUS

Jigger, Arsenius (author of *Magical Drafts and Potions*): Arsenic is a poison used in many magical concoctions. A jigger is a liquid measurement, a bit more than an ounce.

Skeeter, Rita: Fitting for an annoying (and blood-sucking) bug one wants to swat!

Spore, Phyllida (author of *One Thousand Magical Herbs*): From the "spores" plants use as seeds, and the Greek *phylum*, meaning "leaves."

Diagon Alley: Typical of everything in the wizard world, this street doesn't run straight; it runs "diagonally."

Knockturn Alley: This unsavory street, where shops like Borgin & Burkes cater to those who pursue the Dark Arts, is a place you wouldn't want to visit "nocturnally."

Besides Mail, What Does the Arrival of an Owl Mean?

O WLS, OF COURSE, ARE THE PRIMARY
means of communication between wizards in Harry's world. But in our world, even though everyone likes to get mail, not everyone welcomes owls. Many cultures, such as Egyptian, Roman, and Aztec, were ambivalent about this bird of prey. In several parts of the world an owl's screech is considered a bad omen, perhaps even of death. As well, owls, being nocturnal, have long been associated with sorcery, which is always certain to scare someone.

Owls

J. K. Rowling says she found the name for **Hedwig**, Harry's owl, in a book of saints (see **Names**).

Nonetheless, some cultures embraced this bird. The emblem of Athens was an owl, because so many lived there. There was an ancient saying, "Don't send owls to Athens," referring to a silly waste of effort. Today one might hear a similar phrase, "Don't carry coal to Newcastle," because Newcastle is an English coal-mining town.

Because Athens was a center of learning, owls also came to symbolize intelligence. They were even adopted as the emblem of Minerva, Roman goddess of wisdom (counterpart to the Greek goddess Athena, patron of Athens).

What Makes Harry a Universal Hero?

THE DETAILS OF HARRY'S LIFE ARE WELL known to his fans. Some of them have even deduced facts J. K. Rowling leaves out, such the year he was born (see sidebar).

HARRY THE HERO

But if we understand Harry's character deeply, it is not solely because of the facts. It seems that Harry, for all his unique qualities, is a very familiar hero. He is, from the very start of *Stone*, what readers might call a legendary Lost Prince or Hidden Monarch—just like Oedipus, Moses, King Arthur, and countless others in every culture. He never knew he was a wizard—or even that the magical world existed—before receiving the letter inviting him to Hogwarts.

Making him even more familiar, he is, at least by the Dursleys' strange standards, an Ugly Duckling. They think everything about him is odd. So they treat him as Cinderella

Potter, Harry

When Was Harry Born?

Some fans say 1980, calculating from the 500th Deathday of Nearly Headless Nick in *Stone*. Nick died in 1492, dating the *Stone* adventure in 1992. Harry is 12 at the time. Though smaller details in the book contradict this conclusion, it is still a likely guess.

was treated, imprisoning him in a world far less interesting than his birthright, forcing him to sleep under stairs when a four-poster bed awaits him at Hogwarts, and feeding him scraps, which makes him astounded at the abundance of Hogwarts feasts.

HOW HARRY SEES HIMSELF

Though Harry's introduction to the wizard world instantly offers the recognition he so desperately craves—everybody he meets has already heard of "the great Harry Potter"—he still feels self-doubt. The lightning scar is not the only mark Voldemort left. There was a deeper consequence to that battle. Some of Voldemort's psyche found its way into Harry. He worries about the question that stumped the Sorting Hat early in *Stone*: Is he a Gryffindor, with the virtues that implies, or is he a Slytherin, susceptible to evil? In *Chamber*, Dumbledore explains a view of good and evil that has shades of gray, not just dark and light. The bit of Voldemort in Harry, he explains, simply makes him less conventional and more resourceful than the average Gryffindor. It also helps him understand Voldemort, which is an advantage. In future battles, this extra strength and knowledge will undoubtedly help Harry.

Contact with Voldemort made Harry a **parselmouth**, able to speak with snakes.

BLOODLINES

Harry's mother, though a powerful witch, was Muggle-born. For those who care about bloodlines, like Draco Malfoy, Harry's status is inferior. But Harry seems, if anything, stronger for coming from mixed blood.

In fact, his conversations with Draco echo an incident in the childhood of another great British wizard, Merlin, recounted by the early historian Geoffrey of Monmouth: "A sudden quarrel broke out between two of the lads, whose names were Merlin and Dinabutius. As they argued, Dinabutius said to Merlin: 'Why do you try to compete with me, fathead? How can we two be equal in skill? I myself am of royal blood on both sides of my family. As for you, nobody knows who you are, for you never had a father!'"

But Merlin's nemesis, like Draco Malfoy, had a knack for prideful mistakes. His outburst attracted the attention of messengers for King Vortigern, who had been told to find a boy with no father. The young Merlin was brought to the king, and his career began that day.

THE HARRY WITH A THOUSAND FACES

Harry's adventures also follow a familiar pattern. Scholar Joseph Campbell wrote at length about "The Hero with a Thousand Faces," the common character central to cultures all over the world. From Ulysses of ancient Greek myth to Luke Skywalker of *Star Wars*, these heroes and their legends bear a striking similarity. Harry makes it a thousand and one.

Campbell summarized those stories this way: "A hero ventures forth from the world of common day into a region of supernatural wonder. Fabulous forces are there encountered and decisive victory is won. The hero comes back from this mysterious adventure with the power to bestow boons on his fellow man."

The hero's journey has three stages, which Campbell labels *Departure*, *Initiation*, and *Return*. Within those stages are common themes. A glance at any of the books reveals evidence of the pattern:

I. Departure
The hero is called to adventure.
As Campbell describes it, the hero is first seen in our everyday world. He is beginning a new stage in life. A herald may arrive to announce that destiny has summoned the hero.

The very start of *Stone* fits this design. Harry is suffering a dreary life with the Dursleys when he learns a place is waiting for him at Hogwarts. Because the Dursleys have intercepted previous letters, Hagrid arrives to collect him.

Harry continues to spend summers with the Dursleys, so later books also begin with Harry in the ordinary world.

The hero may refuse the call to adventure. He may have any number of reasons, from everyday responsibilities to a selfish refusal to help others. But if he does, he will find that he has no choice in the matter.

Although Harry does not go through this step in *Stone*, he does in later books.

In *Chamber* he is annoyed by the public attention his earlier adventure has created, and craves anonymity. But his intrepid character makes it impossible for him to ignore the mysterious occurrences—which, as destiny would have it, are directed at him.

In *Goblet*, even though he decides not to trick the Goblet of Fire into accepting his entry for the Triwizard Tournament, it selects him anyway.

The hero meets a protector and guide who offers supernatural aid, often in the form of amulets.

This occurs again and again. In *Stone*, Hagrid has been one of Harry's protectors since birth. He was the wizard who first took Harry to the Dursleys when Harry was a baby. Soon after they meet again, when Harry is on his way to Hogwarts, they visit Diagon Alley, where Hagrid arranges for Harry to buy a wand and other wizarding supplies. As a birthday present, Hagrid also gives him an owl, Hedwig. As well, Dumbledore has been a protector and guide. In *Stone*, he gives Harry the invisibility cloak. And in *Azkaban*, Harry learns that Sirius has been protecting him.

The hero encounters the first threshold to a new world. The protector can only lead the hero to the threshold; the hero must cross it alone. He may first have to fight or outwit a guardian of the threshold who wants to prevent the crossing.

The climax of each of Harry's adventures begins with a solitary journey past a threshold.

In *Stone*, Ron can help Harry figure out the right chess moves, and Hermione can help Harry figure out which potions will get him through the black flames; but only Harry can go into "the last chamber," where he confronts Quirrell.

In *Chamber*, although he and Ron and Lockhart all travel down the drain to face the basilisk and save Ginny Weasley, Harry must

In **Alice in Wonderland**, Alice also faces a challenging chess match.

make the final portion of the dangerous journey alone.

The hero enters "the Belly of the Whale," a phrase drawn from legends like the story of Jonah to signify being swallowed into the unknown.

Whether he plunges into the Chamber of Secrets or sneaks into Lupin's hideaway under the Whomping Willow, Harry is in "the Belly of the Whale."

II. Initiation

The hero follows a road of trials. The setting is unfamiliar. The hero may encounter companions who assist him in these trials. Invisible forces may also aid him.

These themes reappear in each book. Harry receives new amulets each time, such as the invisibility cloak in *Stone* and the Marauder's Map in *Azkaban*. He learns how to call on forces such as his Patronus.

Harry's **Patronus** appears as a stag, because that was his father's Animagus form.

The hero is abducted or must take a journey at night or by sea.

Harry is literally kidnapped when he touches the Goblet of Fire, which has been turned into a portkey.

The hero fights a symbolic dragon. He may suffer a ritual death, perhaps even dismemberment.

Harry battles a basilisk, Dementors, and, of course, the greatest symbolic dragon of all—Voldemort.

And it seems that in each adventure Harry suffers new, crippling injuries—for instance, he is literally dismembered in *Chamber*, when his arm breaks during the Quidditch match and his bones are accidentally removed with an incompetent spell.

The hero is recognized by or reunited with his father. He comes to understand this source of control over his life.

In every adventure Harry experiences a deeply touching moment of contact with his parents, such as when they appear in the Mirror of Erised in *Stone* and as ghost images released from Voldemort's wand in *Goblet*.

The hero becomes nearly divine. He has traveled past ignorance and fear.

Harry conquers fear in each adventure. Though he seems surprised to do so again and again, he has a sense, which grows after each confrontation with Voldemort, that the Dark Lord will not defeat him. As Dumbledore says at the end of *Goblet*, "You have shouldered a grown wizard's burden and found yourself equal to it."

The hero receives "the ultimate boon," the goal of his quest. It may be an elixir of life. It may be different than the hero's original goal because he is wiser.

In *Stone*, the Mirror of Erised places "the ultimate boon"—which in fact does make an elixir of life—right in his pocket.

In *Chamber*, he defeats the monster that has lived underneath Hogwarts for decades, saving Ginny Weasley (and countless other students who might have become the basilisk's victims).

In *Azkaban*, he "finds" the prize all the wizards are seeking: Sirius Black. But having learned the truth about Black, he finds a way to spare him an apparently inevitable death sentence—just as if he had given him an elixir of life.

In *Goblet*, the goal is obvious: the victory in the Triwizard Tournament. But what Harry discovers is much deeper. He fights Voldemort wand-to-wand, and escapes death again—this time by virtue of his own skills. He begins to realize just how powerful a wizard he is.

III. Return

The hero takes a "magic flight" back to his original world. He may be rescued by magical forces. One of his original protectors may aid him. A person or thing from his original world may appear to bring him back.

Harry is miraculously saved in *Stone*, and travels back while still unconscious.

In *Chamber*, he is rescued by Fawkes. The phoenix brings the Sorting Hat to deliver Gryffindor's sword, then attacks the basilisk.

In *Goblet*, speaking to the image of Cedric Diggory released from Voldemort's wand, Harry makes a solemn commitment to return Diggory's body to Hogwarts.

The hero crosses the return threshold. He may have difficulty adjusting to his original life, where people will not fully comprehend his experience.

After each school year he must return to the Dursley home on Privet Drive, where understanding is impossible. Even other wizards have trouble comprehending, as described at the end of *Azkaban*: "Nobody at Hogwarts now knew the truth of what had happened. . . . As the end of term approached, Harry heard many different theories about what had really happened, but none of them came close to the truth."

The hero becomes master of two worlds: the everyday world, which represents his material existence; and the magical world, which signifies his inner self.

Simply being in the presence of Voldemort is the worst nightmare of most wizards. But Harry has been there often, seeing things no other wizard has seen. These encounters have made him aware of a part of his psyche that other wizards never consider. One can be sure that eventually—even if he is doubtful—these experiences will help him become a greater wizard than even Dumbledore. (No doubt Dumbledore is aware of this, and pleased by it.)

The hero has won the freedom to live. He has conquered the fears that prevent him from living fully.

Fear, we are told, is Harry's greatest enemy—even greater than Voldemort. In *Azkaban*, Professor Lupin did not let Harry practice fighting the boggart because he did not want an image of Voldemort flying through Hogwarts. But Harry tells him, "I didn't think of Voldemort . . . I remembered those Dementors." Lupin is impressed by Harry's insight. "That suggests that what you fear most of all is fear. Very wise, Harry."

Of course, Rowling does not follow a step-by-step diagram. These patterns appear in each of her books, as they have in mythology and folklore for centuries, because the quest of heroes stays the same. To battle the dark forces in the world, heroes must face the dark forces within, and rediscover in each adventure that they are worthy of victory. We understand Harry because, as Campbell says, "every one of us shares the supreme ordeal."

See also:

Dumbledore

Voldemort

What Are the "Runes" on the Pensieve?

Runes

DUMBLEDORE HAS SO MANY MEMORIES HE stores some in a pensieve, "a shallow stone basin" with "odd carvings around the edge." J. K. Rowling created the name from the French word *penser* ("to think") and *sieve*, which is a tool used to strain liquids and separate out desired things.

Harry recognizes some of the carvings as runes. So what are runes, and why would they belong on a pensieve?

Runes were the first alphabet of the tribes of northern Europe, used in Britain, Scandinavia, and Iceland. They appeared about the third century A.D. and endured more than a millennium. The first six letters were f, u, th, a, r, and k, so the alphabet is sometimes called "futhark."

Rûn is Gaelic for "secret," and *helrûn* means "divination," suggesting that the alphabet was used in magic rituals. They are said to come from the gods themselves. Odin hanged

Viking **runes** carved on a rock.

himself for nine days from Yggdrasil, the great ash tree that holds earth, heaven, and hell, to earn knowledge of the runes. Odin's sacrifice to gain knowledge for humankind symbolizes how greatly learning was valued. In fact, when runes were first used there was little distinction between scholars and wizards. Runes were sometimes used for divination, and in recent years this practice has become popular again. Their symbols are read the way some fortune-tellers read tarot cards.

Runes appear often in J. R. R. Tolkien's *The Lord of the Rings*. The all-important ring mentioned in the title is engraved with a runic message. Tolkien, who loved creating new words as much as J. K. Rowling does, created an entire runic alphabet and language.

See also:
Divination

A tablet carved
with runes, from
about 1000 A.D.

Why Does the Sphinx Ask Harry a Question?

DURING THE THIRD TASK OF THE Triwizard Tournament in *Goblet*, as he nears the center of the maze, Harry meets a Sphinx—"an extraordinary creature," part lion and part woman, with "long, almond-shaped eyes." She tells him, "You are very near your goal. The quickest way is past me." But instead of fighting her, as he would a dragon, he must answer a question.

Sphinx

EGYPTIAN ORIGINS

The Sphinx is a creature from Egyptian mythology. The huge stone sculpture of the Great Sphinx in the Egyptian desert at Giza, built about 2500 B.C., is evidence of the creature's ancient origins and importance. Thousands of smaller Sphinxes were built around Egypt, occasionally with heads modeled on birds of prey.

The face on the Great Sphinx at Giza was actually modeled on a king of Egypt.

In the thousand years after the Great Sphinx was built, the legends of the creature

The Sphinx's strange form and enigmatic manner make it the very symbol of mystery. William Shakespeare once asked, "is not Love . . . subtle as a Sphinx?" *Love's Labours Lost* (act iv, scene iii).

moved to Greece. There it was described as having wings.

THE SPHINX OF THEBES

A particular Sphinx of Greek legend is especially well known. It was sent by the goddess Hera to punish Laius, the king of Thebes, who had kidnapped a young man. That Sphinx challenged travelers on the road to Thebes with a three-part riddle similar to the one Harry was asked to solve:

> *What animal goes on four feet in*
>   *the morning,*
> *Two at noon,*
> *And three in the evening?*

Any traveler was permitted to turn back without answering; but the Sphinx killed anyone who answered incorrectly. One day it was approached by

a young man named Oedipus. He happened
to be Laius's son and heir. (But, like Harry, he
was unaware of his noble origins.) Oedipus
displayed his exceptional qualities by answering the riddle correctly: "Man creeps on
hands and knees in childhood, walks upright
in adulthood, and in old age uses a cane."
Having been bested, the Sphinx killed herself.

See also:
Beasts
Centaurs
Fluffy
Mazes

How Do You Scare a Spider?

ALL SORTS OF SPIDERS—SOME ORDINARY, some unusual—live near Hogwarts. Most of them are common and harmless. A few, like Aragog, Mosag, and their children, are huge, intelligent, and gifted with speech.

Spiders

ARAGOG'S NAME
The source of Aragog's name is the same as the source of "arachnid," the scientific name for spiders. They both come from a mythical woman, Arachne, who was especially gifted in spinning and weaving. Being a bit too proud, Arachne challenged Minerva, Roman goddess of handicrafts, to a contest. Arachne beat

Minerva, but the goddess was so annoyed that she turned Arachne into a spider, forcing her to weave only webs. The names Aragog and Mosag also echo the names of the giants Gog and Magog. As well, *mosag* is a Gaelic word meaning "dirty woman." And in what is probably just a nice coincidence, it's also nearly an anagram of "gossamer"—something light as air, like a spider's web.

The goddess **Minerva**.

MAN-EATERS

In *Chamber*, Aragog seems perfectly willing to let his children eat Ron and Harry. He is following a long tradition. Many authors have enjoyed creating man-eating monsters out of spiders. By comparison, J. K. Rowling's spiders, though perfectly happy to eat humans, seem more understanding than most. They're much kinder than Shelob, the one created by J. R. R. Tolkien in *Lord of the Rings*:

> There agelong she had dwelt, an evil thing in spider-form. . . . and she served none but herself, drinking the blood of Elves and Men, bloated and grown fat with endless brooding on her feasts, weaving webs of shadow; for all living things were her food, and her vomit darkness. . . .

Little she knew of or cared for towers, or rings, or anything devised by mind or hand, who only desired death for all others, mind and body, and for herself a glut of life, alone, swollen till the mountains could no longer hold her up and the darkness could not contain her.

But that desire was yet far away, and long now had she been hungry, lurking in her den, while the power of Sauron grew, and light and living things forsook his borders; and the city in the valley was dead, and no Elf or Man came near, only the unhappy Orcs. Poor food and wary. But she must eat, and however busily they delved new winding passages from the pass and from their tower, ever she found some way to snare them. But she lusted for sweeter meat.

THE USEFULNESS OF SPIDERS

Aragog and his family are good examples of what seem to be important rules in Harry's world: Appearances can be deceiving; and most creatures (as well as humans) tend to treat others only as badly as they've been treated.

It makes sense that underneath the ugliness and anger of Aragog is a feeling creature that can be good rather than evil. In fact, he gives Harry an important clue to the mystery of the Chamber of Secrets. For a time, Aragog was mistakenly believed to be the monster set free from the chamber fifty years before Harry's adventure. But that monster, says Aragog, was actually "an ancient creature we spiders fear above all others." Harry later learns Aragog is referring to the basilisk; and when he sees spiders fleeing Hogwarts he knows the great snake is loose.

See also:

Basilisk

Why Do Trolls Stink?

TROLLS ARE A RACE OF OGRES—UNPLEASANT in both appearance and personality. In *Stone*, Professor Quirrell, who later claims "a special gift with trolls," secretly lets a mountain troll into Hogwarts: "It was a horrible sight. Twelve feet tall, its skin was a dull, granite gray, its great lumpy body like a boulder with its small bald head perched on top like a coconut. It had short legs thick as tree trunks with flat, horny feet. The smell coming from it was incredible."

Trolls

Legends of trolls originated in Scandinavia, where the creatures alarmed residents of the countryside with their size and magical ability. According to some legends they lived in castles; other stories had them living in underground palaces. They only came out at night, and could be turned into stone by sunlight.

As Scandinavians moved to Britain, trolls tagged along, often making their homes under bridges. That may explain why they reek of sewer water. Certain large rocks in the

British northlands are said to be trolls who stayed out until daybreak.

Their bad reputation among humans is based on a variety of legends. They dislike the noise humans make, so they are often cranky; they snatch women and children; some of them are cannibals.

In *Peer Gynt*, a famous play by Norwegian author Henrik Ibsen, the title character light-heartedly acts like a troll, warning: "I'll come to your bedside at midnight tonight. If you should hear someone hissing and spitting, you mustn't imagine it's only the cat. It's me, lass! I'll drain out your blood in a cup; and your little sister, I'll eat her up."

But one must wonder whether trolls suffer from the same prejudice humans have about giants. Later in Ibsen's play, Peer Gynt actually meets a troll, who tells him, "We troll-folk, my son, are less black than we're painted." Though it is hard to believe that trolls are actually kind, it easy to see they may be no worse than humans. At one point Gynt's friend asks him, "What difference is there 'twixt trolls and men?" Gynt replies, "No difference at all, as it seems to me. Big trolls would roast you and small trolls would claw you; with us it would be likewise, if only men dared."

See also:

Goblins

How Do You Catch a Unicorn?

F EW MAGICAL CREATURES HAVE STRUCK the human imagination as deeply as the elegant unicorn. Even in Harry's wizard world, with so many wondrous beasts, the unicorn is a symbol of the sacred. In *Goblet*, J. K. Rowling describes unicorn foals that are "pure gold," with "silvery" blood. Their coats also turn silver around age two, and they "go pure white" when they mature.

Unicorns

ANCIENT UNICORNS

Unicorns appear in the ancient art and myth of Mesopotamia, China, and India. The Roman naturalist Pliny, relying on reports he had heard, called it "a very ferocious beast, similar in the rest of its body to a horse, with the head of a deer, the feet of an elephant, the tail of a boar, a deep bellowing voice, and a single black horn, two cubits [three feet] in length, standing out in the middle of its forehead."

A traveler from the early 1500s saw two unicorns at the temple of Mecca:

The elder is formed like a colt of thirty months old, and he has a horn in the forehead, which horn is about as long as three arms. The other unicorn is like a colt of one year old, and he has a horn of about one foot long. The color of the said animal resembles that of a dark bay horse, and his head resembles that of a stag; his neck is not very long, and he has some thin and short hair which hangs on one side; his legs are slender and lean like those of a goat; the foot is a little cloven in the fore part, and long and goatlike, and there are some hairs on the hind part of the said legs. Truly this monster must be a very fierce and solitary animal. These two animals were presented to the Sultan of Mecca as the finest things that could be found in the world at the present day, and as the richest treasure ever sent by a king of Ethiopia, that is, by a Moorish king. He made this present in order to secure an alliance with the said Sultan of Mecca.

Pliny reported that the unicorn "cannot be taken alive." William Shakespeare referred to the same elusive nature: "Time's glory is to calm contending kings, to unmask falsehood and bring truth to light . . . to tame the unicorn and lion wild."

Other writers suggest the trick is to bait the unicorn with a young virgin—and although this method has never been successfully employed, it fits with the unicorn's role as a symbol of purity and chastity. Many medieval tapestries portray scenes of unicorns to convey the power of sacred devotion. The Old Testament refers to unicorns several times: "God brought them out of Egypt; he hath as it were the strength of the unicorn" (Numbers 23:22); "His horns are like the horns of unicorns: with them he shall push the people together to the ends of the earth"

(Deuteronomy 33:17); "My horn shall thou exalt like the horn of a unicorn" (Psalms 92:10); "Will the unicorn be willing to serve thee, or abide in thy crib?" (Job 39:9). These references, to some scholars, indicate that the unicorn is actually a symbol of Christ.

MAGICAL HEALING POWER

The unicorn's ability to save one's body as well as one's soul has always been a part of its legend. Ctesias, a Greek physician in the employ of the ruler of Persia around 400 B.C., wrote

Unicorn
appearing on a family crest.

one of the first accounts of the creature:

> There are in India certain wild asses
> which are as large as horses, and larger.
> Their bodies are white, their heads dark
> red, and their eyes dark blue. They have a
> horn on the forehead that is about a foot
> and a half in length. The dust filed from
> this horn is administered in a potion as a
> protection against deadly drugs. The base
> of this horn, for some two hands'-breadth
> above the brow, is pure white; the upper
> part is sharp and of a vivid crimson; and
> the remainder, or middle portion, is
> black. Those who drink out of these
> horns, made into drinking vessels, are not
> subject, they say, to convulsions or to the
> holy disease [epilepsy]. Indeed, they are
> immune even to poisons if either before
> or after swallowing such, they drink
> wine, water, or anything else from these
> beakers.

These medicinal qualities, so important to
the critically ill like Voldemort—who kills a
unicorn in *Stone* to drink its life-sustaining
blood—have long made the unicorn an object
of hunters. But as Firenze the centaur says, "It
is a monstrous thing to slay a unicorn."

See also:

Centaurs

Forest

Who Really Wrote the Book on Divination?

T HE DIVINATION TEXTBOOK USED BY students at Hogwarts—*Unfogging the Future*—was written by a woman named Cassandra Vablatsky. That flamboyant name is perfect for a divination expert. It comes from two prominent people whose lives relate to prophecy and magic.

Vablatsky

In Greek myth, Cassandra was a seer—someone who could see the future. She received that gift from the god Apollo, who loved her. He promised her the gift of prophecy if she would return his feelings. But after being made clairvoyant she changed her mind, so Apollo angrily cursed her by declaring that no one would ever believe her. This caused her a lot of grief.

Cassandra plays a part in the well-known story of the Trojan Horse. Being the daughter of King Priam of Troy, she was in the city when it was attacked by Greek soldiers trying to invade it. After it seemed the Greeks had given up, leaving behind the gift of a large wooden horse, she warned her father not to celebrate too soon—and, most of all, not to bring the horse inside city walls. But because of Apollo's curse, her father did not heed her. Of course, Greek soldiers were hidden inside the horse. They waited until the horse was inside the city and everyone was asleep, then slipped out and took over Troy.

Cassandra Vablatsky's last name is no doubt taken from Helena Petrovna Blavatsky (1831–1891), a founder of the Theosophical Society, whose aims include "investigating unexplained laws of nature and the powers latent in humanity"—in other words, magic.

See also:
Divination
Runes

What Makes Veela Angry?

VEELA, SEDUCTIVE NATURE SPIRITS WHO first appear in *Goblet*, originate in legends of Central Europe. They are beautiful young women—or appear to be such. In some stories they are said to be ghosts of unbaptized women whose souls cannot leave earth. Their beauty is astonishing and can make men act foolishly. They have long hair, so fair it seems white.

Veela

THE DARK SIDE OF VEELA

Veela can be quite jealous. A famous Serbian tale, "Prince Marko and the Veela," tells of an encounter with the veela Ravioyla:

> Two brothers, Duke Milosh and Kralyevich Marko, rode side by side over magnificent Miroch Mountain. As the sun rose, Marko fell asleep, then awoke with a start. "Milosh," he said, "I cannot stay awake. Sing to me to keep from sleeping."
>
> Duke Milosh answered, "Oh, Kralyevich Marko, I cannot sing to you. Last night I drank with the veela Ravioyla, and

drank too much and sang too loudly and too well, and the veela warned me that if I sing on her mountain she will shoot her arrows into me."

Kralyevich Marko replied, "Brother, you cannot be afraid of a veela. I am Kralyevich Marko. With my golden battle-axe, we are both safe." So Milosh sang, telling a story of kings and kingdoms and the glory of our country.

Marko listened, but the song did not keep sleep away. Soon he was dreaming again.

The veela Ravioyla heard Milosh, and she sang back to him in a beautiful voice. But Milosh answered her in a voice that was even finer, and she became angry as she had before. She flew to Miroch Mountain, and expertly drew two arrows at once in her bow. One hit Milosh in the throat, silencing him. The other hit his heart.

Both horses stopped, and Marko awoke. With great effort Milosh was able to speak, but only in a dying whisper. He said to Marko, "Brother! Veela Ravioyla has shot me because I sang on Miroch Mountain."

Veela are also gifted in the healing arts, with a special knowledge of natural remedies. In the story above, the veela Ravioyla heals Milosh and tells other veela not to bother the men. In fact, veela tend to be kind to humans—and are known to marry mortal men. What upsets them most is having their ritual dances disturbed. If that occurs, they may become fiercely angry. As spirits of the wind, veela can invoke whirlwinds and storms as they did during the Quidditch World Cup.

See also:

Cornish Pixies

What Kind of Nightmares Created Voldemort?

NOTHING BRINGS OUT A GREAT HERO AS much as a great villain. Lord Voldemort—the half-Muggle born as Thomas Marvolo Riddle—fits the bill. It is no surprise that wizards call him the Dark Lord. That name describes a whole category of literary villains with whom Voldemort has much in common.

Voldemort

Critics John Clute and John Grant note a few characteristics that make a classic Dark Lord:

- A Dark Lord "has often been already defeated but not destroyed eons before."
- He "aspires to be the Prince of this world."
- He is an "abstract force," less flesh and blood than supernatural energy.
- He represents "thinning," the idea that "before the written story started there was a diminishment" such as the chaos and

death Voldemort caused before Harry was
sent to live with the Dursleys.

- He is also a symbol of "debasement," a
moral collapse, often as a result of a questionable bargain, such as the one struck by
the many Death Eaters who sought to gain
power through their alliance with Voldemort.
- He "inflicts damage out of envy."

By this reckoning, Voldemort is the very
model of a Dark Lord.

Yet for all his similarity to other villains,
Voldemort embodies J. K. Rowling's own definition of evil. His desires say something
specific about society right now, as Rowling
perceives it and writes about it.

VOLDEMORT AND IMMORTALITY

Voldemort leaves no mystery about his intentions. As he tells the Death Eaters who flock
to him at the end of *Goblet*, "You know my
goal—to conquer death."

This matter of immortality is never far
from J. K. Rowling's imagination. The whole
first book is devoted to Voldemort's quest for
the Sorcerer's Stone, an object that will assure
it. "Once I have the Elixir of Life," he says in
Stone, "I will be able to create a body of my

own." And of course he will be able to elude death, as the Flamels have done for hundreds of years.

This lust for eternal life is the essence of the Dark Lord's depravity. But is he really any different from the many people in our world who try to live as long they can? Dumbledore tells Harry, "The Stone was really not such a wonderful thing. As much money and life as you could want! The two things most human beings would choose above all—the trouble is, humans do have a knack of choosing precisely those things that are worst for them." The Flamels had that power, but they did not earn it through evil or use it in a way that harmed others. In every culture, immortality, though desirable, is against the laws of nature. Things must die so other things may be born.

GREED

The laws of nature make it impossible for everyone to be immortal, so it is no surprise Voldemort's goal is for himself alone. He'll repay the Death Eaters in other ways, filling their need for confidence or granting them power.

Though it will cost many lives to achieve his goal, he doesn't hesitate. Other people don't matter to him—especially Muggles.

Because his father abandoned his mother, he hates Muggles with what Rowling herself has called a "racist" passion.

Voldemort does not realize that his selfish ambition throws nature out of balance. But given the state of the world when Rowling conceived of the books—genocidal wars in Africa and the Balkans, war in the Middle East, a widening gap between wealthy and poor nations—one can easily see how Voldemort's personality was developed.

Why Do Wizards Use Wands?

WITHOUT QUESTION, A WAND IS A wizard's most important tool. In Harry's world, they are made by combining parts of magical creatures—such as "unicorn hairs, phoenix tail feathers, and the heart-strings of dragons"—with staffs of willow, mahogany, yew, oak, beech, maple, and ebony. Each wand is not only matched to the personality of the individual, but actually chooses the wizard.

Wands

ANCIENT WANDS

It seems wizards have always used wands. These sticks—or in some cases large rods—focus magical strength.

Some anthropologists believe that Stone Age cave paintings showing people with sticks are meant to portray leaders of the clans holding wands to attest to their power. That is only a guess, but strong evidence goes back at least to the time of ancient Egypt. Hieroglyphs show priests holding small rods. In Greek mythology, Hermes, messenger of the Greek gods, carried a special wand called a

The **Druids** had different wands for each of their seven levels of priesthood.

The Egyptian god Thoth was also pictured carrying an early version of a **caduceus**.

See also:
Druids
Egypt

caduceus. This is a rod with wings, around which two serpents are twisted, meant to signify wisdom and healing powers. Physicians adopted it as their symbol hundreds of years ago and still use it today.

In the past some wizards have favored wands made from the elder tree, which is considered especially magical. Those who practiced dark magic often used cypress, which was associated with death. However, J. K. Rowling tells us Voldemort's wand is made of yew. Yet that also makes sense. The yew has immense supernatural power. At one time the yew was one of the few evergreens in Britain, so it has become a symbol of both death and rebirth—the same immortality Voldemort desperately wants.

Are Any of the "Famous Witches and Wizards" Real?

WHEN THEY FIRST TAKE THE HOGWARTS Express to school, Ron introduces Harry to the Famous Witches and Wizards trading cards that come with Chocolate Frogs. He mentions a few: Dumbledore, Merlin, Paracelsus, the Druidess Cliodna, Hengist of Woodcroft, Morgana, Ptolemy, and Circe. Some of these wizards are actual historical figures. Others exist in legends going back hundreds of years.

Wizards

AGRIPPA

Heinrich Cornelius Agrippa was a wizard during the Renaissance. Born Heinrich Cornelis near Cologne, Germany, in 1486, he took the name Agrippa in honor of the founder of his hometown.

He had a varied career, working as a doctor, lawyer, astrologer, and faith healer. But he made enemies as quickly as friends and was

The magical philosopher Heinrich Cornelius **Agrippa**.

branded a sorcerer. In 1529, he published a book called *On Occult Philosophy*, combining ancient Hebrew and Greek texts to argue that the best way to know God was through magic. The Church deemed him a heretic and jailed him. He died in 1535.

Agrippa was one inspiration for Wolfgang Goethe's play *Faust*, in which a scholar makes a pact with the Devil—similar to the pact between Voldemort and his followers. His name also came to be the term for a special sorcerer's handbook cut into the shape of a person.

Incidentally, his trading card is one of the most rare.

DRUIDESS CLIODNA

In Irish mythology, Cliodna has several roles, from goddess of beauty to ruler of the Land of Promise—the afterlife. She is also goddess of the sea. Some say she is symbolized at the seacoast by every ninth wave that breaks on shore. She has three enchanted birds that heal the sick.

PARACELSUS

Philippus Aureolus Paracelsus, born in Switzerland in 1493, is considered a founder of modern chemistry and medicine. He began his career as a medical doctor, then turned to the study of magic, especially alchemy and divination. His reputation as a wizard and his role as a doctor are linked. Because he refused to limit himself to the traditional medical education of the time and developed his own successful treatments, he was deemed a sorcerer. But Paracelsus ignored his critics. "The universities do not teach all things," he said, "so a doctor must seek out old wives, gypsies, sorcerers, wandering tribes, old robbers, and such outlaws and take lessons from them. A doctor must be a traveler. Knowledge is experience."

Paracelsus developed several useful remedies. He also found the cause of silicosis, a

The gifted doctor
Paracelsus.

miner's disease that comes from inhaling metal vapors, which previously had been blamed on evil spirits. He helped stop an outbreak of the plague in 1534 by using a form of vaccination.

Because of his attitude and accomplishments, other doctors disliked him. He spent almost a decade in academic exile—and was even forced to flee the city of Basel under cover of darkness in 1528. But by the time of his death in 1541 his reputation had improved greatly.

MORGANA

Morgana—sometimes known as Morgan Le Fay—was a powerful enchantress of British myth, especially gifted in the healing arts. Merlin was her tutor, and she is sometimes said to be the half-sister of King Arthur. However, she was often Arthur's rival, stealing his sword Excalibur and plotting his death.

According to some legends she lived in the Straits of Messina, off Italy. An unusual sea current in that area often draws phosphorescent creatures from the depths to the surface, creating the impression of strange lights or objects floating above the water. These are called Fata Morgana, from *fata*, the Italian word for fairy.

MERLIN

Merlin is considered one of the wisest wizards ever. A master sorcerer, he was said to have been an advisor to the British kings Vortigern, Uther Pendragon, and Arthur. Although he may have been based on a wizard who actually lived, the Merlin we know is a character created from fantastic legends. For instance, some say he arranged the huge stones at Stonehenge. Others say he was gifted in prophecy because he lived backward, so he had already seen the future.

He is best known as King Arthur's mentor. In a noteworthy parallel, he hid the infant Arthur just as Dumbledore knew to hide Harry from Voldemort. The poet Alfred Lord Tennyson recounted that part of the legend in *Idylls of the King*:

> *By reason of the bitterness and grief*
> *That vext his mother, all before his time*
> *Was Arthur born, and all as soon as born*
> *Delivered at a secret postern-gate*
> *To Merlin, to be holden far apart*
> *Until his hour should come; because the lords*
> *Of that fierce day were as the lords of this,*
> *Wild beasts, and surely would have torn*
> *   the child*
> *Piecemeal among them, had they known;*
> *   for each*
> *But sought to rule for his own self and hand,*
> *And many hated Uther.*
> *Wherefore Merlin took the child,*
> *And gave him to Sir Anton, an old knight*
> *And ancient friend of Uther; and his wife*
> *Nursed the young prince, and reared him with*
> *   her own;*
> *And no man knew. And ever since the lords*
> *Have fought like wild beasts among themselves,*
> *So that the realm has gone to wrack.*

Merlin then became both Arthur's tutor and his counselor, using his keen intelligence and innumerable acts of wizardry to help the young king fight Britain's enemies.

According to some stories, Merlin was tricked by the Lady of the Lake, whom he loved, into creating a magical column of air that she then used to imprison him forever.

HENGIST OF WOODCROFT

This wizard either is or is named for a Saxon king of Britain. King Hengist and his brother Horsa—their names come from the German words for "stallion" and "horse"—arrived in Britain in A.D. 449 as mercenaries to help King Vortigern put down Pict and Scot rebels, but they eventually led a rebellion of their own. Hengist founded the kingdom of Kent.

Though not referred to as Hengist of Woodcroft in the Anglo-Saxon Chronicles, under questioning by Vortigern he proclaimed, "We worship the gods of our own country: Saturn, Jove and the others who rule over this world, and more especially Mercury, whom in our language we call Woden. Our ancestors dedicated the fourth day of the week to him, and down to our time that day is called Wednesday from his name." It is reasonable to guess Hengist might also name his estate for Woden.

More likely, the name Woodcroft is simply one that J. K. Rowling spotted on a map and liked. In Peterborough, England, north of Kent, one does find a Woodcroft Castle, site of a grisly murder and an old ghost. In 1648 Dr. Michael Hudson, chaplain to King Charles, was killed there while battling Oliver Cromwell's troops. He is said to haunt the castle on the anniversary of his death. Sounds of the battle can be heard, as well as Hudson's cries for mercy.

J. K. Rowling says she often finds names on maps (see **Names**).

CIRCE

In Homer's ancient epic poem *The Odyssey*, Circe is a "great and cunning goddess" who lives on an island. Odysseus's men, returning home after the Trojan War, stop at her island and become victims of this enchantress:

> When they reached Circe's house they found it built of cut stones, on a site that could be seen from far, in the middle of the forest. There were wild mountain wolves and lions prowling all round it— poor bewitched creatures whom she had tamed by her enchantments and drugged into subjection. Presently they reached

the gates of the goddess's house, and as they stood there they could hear Circe within, singing most beautifully as she worked at her loom, making a web so fine, so soft, and of such dazzling colors as no one but a goddess could weave. They called her and she came down, unfastened the door, and bade them enter. They, thinking no evil, followed her.

When she had got them into her house, she set them upon benches and seats and mixed them a drink with honey, but she drugged it with wicked poisons to make them forget their homes, and when they had drunk she turned them into pigs by a stroke of her wand, and shut them up in her pigsties. They were like pigs—head, hair, and all—and they grunted just as pigs do; but their senses were the same as before, and they remembered everything.

Odysseus himself, having taken a special potion, resists Circe's charms and eventually frees his men.

PTOLEMY

Claudius Ptolemaeus lived in Alexandria, Egypt, in the early part of the second century

A.D., where he was an astronomer and mathematician. He collected the world's knowledge of those fields into a book, eventually known as the *Almagest*, which influenced scholars for more than a thousand years. His most significant conclusion was that the Earth is the center of the universe, and that all other celestial bodies revolve around it. This is known as the "Ptolemaic system." Although it was disproved in the 1500s by the astronomer Nicolaus Copernicus, Ptolemy's records of his observations of the heavens are still considered useful to scholars even if his conclusions are not.

ALBERIC GRUNNION

This name must have been inspired by the Alberich who is a powerful wizard in the German epic poem *Nibelungenlied* ("Song of the Nibelungen"). The poem is a mythical account of a historical event, the defeat by the Huns of the kingdom of Burgundy (now part of France) in A.D. 437. It has been the basis of many modern works, most importantly the Ring Cycle, a series of linked operas written in the nineteenth century by Richard Wagner. (When you see cartoons of opera singers wearing horned helmets, it is Wagner's Ring Cycle they're singing.)

The name Oberon, which William Shakespeare gave to the king of the fairies in *Midsummer Night's Dream*, is an English form of Alberich.

In Wagner's version of the story, Alberich is king of the dwarves, full of hate and ambition. When he discovers a hoard of gold guarded by unsuspecting maidens, he does not hesitate to swear off love forever to win it. He uses the gold to make a ring that gives him great power. When the ring is stolen from him, he places a curse on it. Anyone else who wears it will suffer greatly. As the story goes on, others try to win the ring, paying the price for their desire.

One hero of the Ring Cycle wins a prize from Alberich that will be familiar to Harry Potter fans: an **invisibility cloak**!

See also:
Flamel

Afterword

E VERY WRITER BEGINS AS A READER. AFTER DIGGING INTO her stories, one sees that J. K. Rowling must have been a terrific reader before she became a terrific writer. Just as impressive as her knowledge of myths and legends is her ability to make each one seem original and fresh.

In the bibliography of this book, as well as in the notes for each entry, you'll find suggestions of interesting books for further reading. The best place to start would certainly be a collection of Greek and Roman myths. If you want to dig deeper, an outstanding reference with many detailed reading suggestions is *The Encyclopedia of Fantasy* by John Clute and John Grant. If you're particularly interested in magical creatures, you'll like Carol Rose's encyclopedias, *Giants, Monsters and Dragons* and *Spirits, Fairies, Leprechauns and Goblins*. For information about wizards, good sources are Rosemary Ellen Guiley's *The Encyclopedia of Witches and Witchcraft* and Thomas Ogden's *Wizards and*

Sorcerers. You might also want to find the wonderful *Dictionary of Imaginary Places*, by Alberto Manguel and Gianni Guadalupi. Many books explain people and creatures, but this may be the only one that brings together fantastic worlds.

As most readers already know, the Internet is full of information about the Harry Potter books. For instance, a few websites are devoted entirely to the meanings behind the names J. K. Rowling creates. Others, like Bartleby.com, offer a thorough background on mythology. Some web addresses are listed in the bibliography.

Whatever you read while you're waiting for the next Harry Potter—or whatever you write—you're bound to uncover connections between Harry's world and the many magical worlds J. K. Rowling discovered before she created Harry. They stayed with her, and they'll stay with you, too.

Acknowledgments

Once again, having a family of professional writers and editors has proven crucial. I'm grateful to my parents and sisters for their expert advice and many hours of reading. Lena Tabori's advice and effort were also essential. Special thanks also to Laurie Brown, Max and Emily de La Bruyère, Linda Dudajek and Debbie Malicoat of R. R. Donnelley, Natasha Tabori Fried, Katie Kerr, Lyuba Konopasek, Miles Kronby, Arif Lalani, my copyeditor Laura Poole of Archer Editorial Services, Edward Samuels, Stacy Schiff, Ben Shykind, John Ward of Ward & Olivo, Terry Wybel and the staff of Continental Sales, and the staff of Bristol Books in Wilmington, North Carolina.

Bibliography

Borges, Jorge Luis, with Margarita Guerrero. *The Book of Imaginary Beings* (New York: Dutton, 1969).

Campbell, Joseph. *The Hero with a Thousand Faces* (Princeton: Princeton University Press, 1968).

Clute, John, and John Grant. *The Encyclopedia of Fantasy* (New York: St. Martin's, 1999).

Foster, Robert. *The Complete Guide to Middle-earth* (New York: Ballantine, 1979).

Guiley, Rosemary Ellen. *The Encyclopedia of Witches and Witchcraft* (New York: Facts on File, 1999).

Helms, Randel. *Tolkien's World* (Boston: Houghton Mifflin, 1974).

Le Guin, Ursula K. *A Wizard of Earthsea* (Berkeley, California: Parnassus Press, 1968).

Nigg, Joseph. *The Book of Fabulous Beasts: A Treasury of Writings from Ancient Times to the Present* (New York: Oxford University Press, 1999).

Ogden, Tom. *Wizards and Sorcerers: from Abracadabra to Zoroaster* (New York: Facts on File: 1977).

Rose, Carol. *Giants, Monsters, and Dragons: An Encyclopedia of Folklore, Legend, and Myth* (Santa Barbara, California: ABC-CLIO, 2000).

Rose, Carol. *Spirits, Fairies, Leprechauns, and Goblins: An Encyclopedia* (New York: Norton, 1998).

Tolkien, J. R. R. *The Lord of the Rings* (Boston: Houghton Mifflin, 1965).

White, T. H. *The Sword in the Stone* (New York: Putnam's, 1939).

Willis, Roy. *Dictionary of World Myth* (London: Duncan Baird, 1995).

Internet Resources of interest:

Rudolf Hein's "Do You Know Mundungus Fletcher?"
http://www.rudihein.de/hpewords.htm

Ellie Rosenthal's "What's in a Name?
http://www.stas.net/5/wian/

The Encyclopaedia Potterica
http://www.geocities.com/EnchantedForest/1900/index.html

Notes

In most cases, reference is made in the text to the original source. For classic texts such as *The Odyssey*, interested readers will find many excellent translations and editions. Here is further information:

Introduction
page 16: "go ahead and look it up": online chat at Barnes & Noble.com (www.bn.com), October 20, 2000.

page 16: "it's the sort of touch": "Wild About Harry," TIME, 20 September 1999, Paul Gray, Elizabeth Gleick, Andrea Sachs.

page 16: "cauldron of story": from the essay "On Fairy-Stories" (1938), quoted in Helms, Randel, *Tolkien's World* (Boston: Houghton, 1974).

Animagus
page 28: "I personally would like to think:"online chat at America Online, 19 October 2000.

Black, Sirius
page 44: "home of departed souls": Temple, Robert K. G., *The Sirius Mystery* (Rochester: Destiny Books, 1976).

page 45: "guide ways for the soul": Lamy, Lucie, *Egyptian Mysteries* (New York: Crossroad, 1981).

page: 46: quotations regarding black dogs: G. MacEwan, *Mystery Animals of Britain and Ireland* (London: Robert Hale, 1968); Bord, J. and Bord, C., *Alien Animals* (London: Panther Books, 1985). Cited at website of Simon Sherwood, Ph.D. candidate, University of Edinburgh department of psychology: http://moebius.psy.ed.ac.uk/ ~simon

Broomsticks
page 49: Holmes: from *The Broomstick Train*, 1891.

Dementors
page 57: "That is exactly": interview with Ann Treneman, *The Times* (London),
    30 June 2000.

Dragons
page 61: "to kill a dragon": Clute, John, and John Grant, *The Encyclopedia of
    Fantasy* (New York: St. Martin's, 1999).
page 62: "the dragon is the largest of all serpents": from Isidore of Seville,
    Etymologies, quoted in Nigg, Joseph, *The Book of Fabulous Beasts* (New
    York: Oxford, 1999).
page 62: "The dragon had the trade-mark": from the essay "On Fairy-Stories"
    (1938), quoted in Helms, Randel, *Tolkien's World* (Boston: Houghton,
    1974).
page 63: "began with ominous signs": *Anglo-Saxon Chronicle*, quoted in Nigg.
page 65: "there is cut out of a dragon's brain": Solinus, *Collection of Remarkable
    Facts*, quoted in Nigg.

Egypt
page 79: "He who is a priest": quoted by Michael Poe, www.sibyllinewicca.org/
    lib_historical/ lib_h_egypt4.htm

Fawkes
page 81: "how many creatures": Ovid, *Metamorphoses* (New York: Viking, 1958).

Flamel
page 86: "finally I found": Flamel, Nicholas, *Testament of Nicolas Flamel*, quoted
    in Askin, Wade, *The Sorcerer's Handbook* (New York: Philosophical
    Library, 1974).

Giants
page 95: "If you want to grace the burial place": Geoffrey of Monmouth,
    History of the Kings of Britain (New York: E.P. Dutton 1958).

Goblins
page 95: "were bred in mockery of Elves": Foster, Robert, *The Complete Guide to
    Middle-earth* (New York: Ballantine, 1978) p. 388.

Griffins
page 107: "I have heard": Aelian, *On Animals*, quoted in Nigg.
page 109: "A fabulous animal": Biedermann, Hans, *Dictionary of Symbolism*
    (Meridian, 1994).
page 110: "The griffin is very popular": Franklyn, Julian, Shield and Crest (New
    York: Sterling, 1961).

Hogwarts

page 117: "Here are all the rites": from "The Playing Fields of Hogwarts," *The New York Times*, 10 October 1999.

Latin

page 124: "I like to think": online chat at Barnes & Noble.com (www.bn.com), 20 October 2000.

Manticore

page 131: "There is in India": Aelian, *On Animals*, quoted in Nigg.

Merpeople

page 139: "I fancied you": Hawthorne, Nathaniel, "The Village Uncle," in *Twice-Told Tales* (Boston: Ticknor, 1849).

Mirrors

page 141: "Buy a looking glass": *The Encyclopedia of Witches and Witchcraft* (New York: Facts on File, 1999).

Unicorns

page 180: "The elder is formed": *The Travels of Ludovico de Varthenta in Egypt, Arabia Deserta and Arabia Felix, in Persia, India, and Ethiopia* (London: Hakluyt Society, 1863), quoted in Nigg.
page 181: "time's glory:" Shakespeare, *The Rape of Lucrece*.
page 183: "There are in India certain wild asses": Ctesias, *Indica*.

Veela

page 187: "Two blood brothers": adapted from Low, David H. (trans.), *The Ballads of Marko Kraljevic* (New York: Greenwood, 1968).

Voldemort

page 191: "A Dark Lord has often been": see entry for "Dark Lord" in Clute, John, *The Encyclopedia of Fantasy* (New York: St. Martin's, 1999) p. 250.
page 194: "racist": TIME, 30 October, 2000.

All illustrations come from the Dover Publication art collection except for those on pages 22, 93, 117, 160, 167, 168, 174 (from www.arttoday.com) and pages 52 and 200 (reproduced with slight alteration from Ogden, Tom, *Wizards and Sorcerers: from Abracadabra to Zoroaster*. New York: Facts on File: 1997).

Index

About the Author

Formerly a head writer of television's *Who Wants To Be a Millionaire* and an editorial director of HarperCollins, David Colbert is best known as author of the acclaimed *Eyewitness* history series. The first of those volumes, *Eyewitness to America*, was a Main Selection of Book-of-the-Month Club and the History Book Club; the latest, *Eyewitness to Wall Street*, will be published in 2001 by Random House's Broadway Books. He is also the editor of Time-LIFE's *Baseball: The National Pastime in Art and Literature* and the forthcoming *World War II: A Tribute in Art and Literature*. A graduate of Brown University, he studied anthropology and mythology but spent most of his time reading randomly in the library, which is pretty much what he still does. He lives in North Carolina and can be contacted at djcolbert@aol.com.